CONSTRUCTION
GENIUS

CONSTRUCTION
GENIUS

Effective, Hands-On, Practical, Simple, No-BS Leadership, Strategy, Sales, and Marketing Advice for Construction Companies

ERIC ANDERTON

ABC Group
Sacramento, CA

Construction Genius copyright © 2022 by Eric Anderton

Caradog E. Anderton
ABC Group
9137 Vancouver Drive
Sacramento, CA 95826
Send feedback to eric@constructiongenius.com

Publisher's Cataloging-In-Publication Data

Names: Anderton, Eric, author.
Title: Construction genius : effective, hands-on, practical, simple, no-BS leadership, strategy, sales, and marketing advice for construction companies / Eric Anderton.
Description: Sacramento, CA : Caradog E. Anderton, [2022]
Identifiers: ISBN: 979-8-9864333-0-1 (hardcover) | 979-8-9864333-1-8 (softcover) | 979-8-9864333-2-5 (ebook) | 979-8-9864333-3-2 (audiobook)
Subjects: LCSH: Construction industry--Management. | Leadership. | Selling. | Strategic planning. | Business communication. | Success in business.
Classification: LCC: HD9715.A2 A54 2022 | DDC: 624.068--dc23

Special discounts for bulk sales are available.
Please contact eric@constructiongenius.com.

This book is dedicated to the construction company owners, executives, and leaders who commit themselves to providing for their families, improving the lives of their employees, and enhancing their communities. Construction is essential, and without you, we would not enjoy the structures and infrastructures that make life easier. Thank you!

Contents

Tell Me What You Think

Let other readers know what you thought of *Construction Genius*. Please write an honest review for this book on your favorite online bookshop.

★ ★ ★ ★ ★

Get Your Exclusive Bonus Chapter

By buying this book, you've already unlocked an exclusive bonus chapter—Chapter 13: How to Start (or Restart) a Construction Company. This bonus chapter is available only on my Construction Genius website. Visit www.ConstructionGenius.com/BonusChapter.

Aside from the secret chapter, my site also offers the most up-to-date construction leadership, strategy, and sales and marketing content to keep you on top of your game for the rest of your career.

You'll also find links to contact me, follow me on social media, and gain new knowledge around the construction industry. I release a lot of podcast episodes to a huge and growing audience. Each episode introduces another expert who can help you maximize your profits while minimizing your burnout. If you're running a construction company, you need every tool you can get. Go to my website and enjoy those free resources, www.ConstructionGenius.com.

CHAPTER 1

EVERY CONSTRUCTION LEADER'S STORY

The first thing I noticed about Dan when our Zoom meeting started was how tired and worried he looked. After some initial pleasantries, I leaned forward.

"Tell me what's on your mind," I said.

"I've been listening to your *Construction Genius* podcast for the last few months," Dan told me, "and it's been so useful that I signed up for the Shift, your online course on leadership. I'm hungry for more because I want to win. I've built my construction company from scratch, but I'm at that tipping point you talked about. My senior leaders and I have to shift from getting stuck in the weeds building projects to leading teams and building people. But I don't know how. I wanted your one-on-one coaching because I have so many questions and frustrations that I've bottled up because I don't have anyone to talk things out with."

"I get it," I said. Dan had a lot to say. Which meant he had a lot he needed someone to hear. Someone who gets it.

"I'm not *just* the CEO," Dan continued. "I'm also the best project manager we have. We've got to win big commercial contracts to grow, but I often find myself talking to the wrong people. I have several project managers now, but my project executives and I end up doing the managers' job—so we never have time to do ours. And I wish I could find a way to make sure new hires are a good fit for my company before I invest in them. I can't grow my company because my project managers aren't competent enough to handle the work. I just—I don't know how to lead them all to do their jobs better." He paused, then blew out a quick sigh. "And I just made the worst mistake of my career."

"What happened?" I asked.

"I spent the last several weeks going after a mall project," Dan replied. "I wanted to make sure the proposal was perfect, so I did every detail myself. But we lost."

"Do you know why?" I said, suspecting I knew the answer.

"I wasn't dealing with the final decision maker," Dan responded. "The guy who got the deal was."

Dan was able to build his construction company to its current level with his skills as a project manager. But now that he had other project managers reporting to him, he didn't know how to lead them as their CEO. He didn't know how to build relationships with key clients. He didn't know how to do the CEO's job of people development, strategic development, and client development so that his company could thrive. He didn't know how to make sure the next generation of leadership would be ready to take over so that he could sell it when he wanted to retire.

"I have some good news for you," I told Dan with a smile. "As you know, you and your project executives are making the shift from being builders of projects to builders of teams and leaders of people. A big role leaders have is fostering long-term relationships with final decision makers at the companies you want as clients. No more chasing lower-level staff for months, with proposals they can't sign off on anyway. I'll also show you a system for hiring people who have the right technical skills and who fit in with the way your company works. What you'll learn will do more than just make your business grow. It will give you back your time to be with your family and have a life."

Dan's face brightened.

"Let's get started," he said.

Just then there was a knock at Dan's door.

"Excuse me for just a sec," Dan said. He stood and opened his door, and I could hear a man's voice describing a problem to Dan and asking for help. Dan gave him a solution to try and then returned to his chair.

"We'll begin with what just happened," I told Dan. "What was that about?"

"Justin had a problem with his client," Dan answered. "He needed me to tell him how to put out the fire. I'm going to have to have a difficult conversation with the client after this meeting. He trusts me."

"Why does your client trust you more than Justin?" I asked.

"I go to the weekly project meetings that my project managers have with their clients," Dan said. "That way I know everything's being done right."

"Dan, I've got some bad news for you," I said.

Dan stiffened. "What's that?"

"When you micromanage your employees, you don't have time to do your job. If you're always the one putting out the fires, Justin can't do his job because he's afraid you'll overrule him. And because you're in the room, the client looks to you instead of him."

"Well, what should I be doing instead?"

"Think about what would happen if you'd said, 'Justin, you figure it out, then come back and tell me your solution.'"

Dan looked astonished. Then his face lit up.

"Justin could solve the problem," Dan answered. "And he'd be a lot happier taking the responsibility."

"Right," I said. "Now what would you do to get his client to bond with him instead of always wanting to talk to you?"

"What if I only went to Justin's client meetings once a month?"

"Try it. Because you're going to need that time to do everything I'm going to teach you. Do you want to learn to lead your teams, develop strategies to guide your marketing and growth, and create relationships with the final decision makers so that you can sell to them?"

"Hell yes!"

"Good." I smiled. "You just aced your first lesson in time management."

Why *Construction Genius*?

Humans are builders. You know the feeling when you drive down the road in your truck, point to a project you recently completed, and say, "I built that"? There's nobility in building things, people, companies, and communities. Building gives our lives great meaning, and if you own or work in a construction company, building is literally what you do.

Yet I've seen too many construction companies that are just getting by. They have no sense of purpose. Their client relationships are weak, their employees are flighty, and their company reputation is fragile. The CEO is stressed, frustrated, and miserable—and so are the employees. A company like that doesn't just affect its workers; it hurts the community.

But it doesn't have to. I want to teach all the Dans of this world to succeed in the construction industry. With my *Construction Genius* podcast, coaching, and classes, I've already helped thousands of clients turn their construction companies around. And with this book, I can help even more.

You see, I understand construction companies—why they fail and what they need to do to succeed. In this book, I'll be sharing systems, tools, and insights that I've developed and tested since 2004 with hundreds of construction companies with revenue from $10 million to $1 billion.

Do they work?

"I was originally hesitant about your Foreman Leadership Academy," wrote Roger Leasure, president of Northern California Tile and Stone, when I asked him about his experience as a coaching client. "Twenty thousand dollars is a lot of money. But with the size of my business and the cost of my payroll, I knew I would make that money back in a matter of months. I justified the expense because the bonding, teamwork, and employee retention was worth it. I was spending money to make money, and after your classes started, I knew it was worth it. You were engaging, and you got the guys to participate. My foremen are opening their eyes to what it takes to run a company with real returns.

"With regard to the executive coaching and advice you've provided me, I liked how specific you were and how you could cut to the chase.

When we first sat down, you asked what I wanted out of our partnership. I told you I didn't want more money, better jobs, or better employees. I wanted time. You immediately said boom, boom, boom, here's your Friday—this is how you do it.

"You gave me clear advice on how to handle employee problems, how to talk to them, and how to hold them accountable. As a result, I saw an employee in a different light instead of having to fire him and pick up the slack myself. Now I'm working on million-dollar jobs instead of doing a one-hundred-thousand-a-year superintendent's job.

"Now I can work *on* my business as opposed to *in* my business. I can look at a work site from a higher view and see the issues from a different perspective. I can ask why my employees are using that small jackhammer when I know for a fact we have a bigger jackhammer that's faster and easier to use. I can tell them to get a golf cart on-site that costs eight thousand dollars but that will save us sixty thousand dollars in man hours.

"I would, without a doubt, recommend working with you. People who work with you are going to increase their personal time and profit. They will increase their employees' knowledge and team building so that they'll have better employee retention and more time."

Keep reading, and I'll teach you to take your construction company to the next level, too.

Become a *Construction Genius* in Three Straightforward Steps

Construction is a risky business. Not because there's a lack of work. It's because the skills that get you to the top aren't the ones that keep you there. Knowing how to build well is where you start. To grow your company requires developing efficient teams, strategic thinking, and building relationships with key clients. That's why this book is divided into three sections: leadership, strategy, and sales/marketing.

I'll teach you how to go from a builder of projects, to a builder of teams, to the leader of a company so successful that you can sell it for a profit.

Step 1: The Shift: Why Leadership First?

Leadership is a loaded word, but I simply think of leadership as people development. We start with developing and perfecting your leadership skills because the success of your construction company is a *direct* reflection of your ability to lead people to execute projects profitably. You won't just learn how to lead your project managers. You'll learn how to teach *them* to become effective leaders, too.

Your new leadership skills will also enable you to track the things you can't control and to make the most of the things you can. This way, you'll learn to ensure your projects are profitable.

Construction has unique challenges that only insiders and experts can understand. Generic leadership training isn't helpful because so much of it simply doesn't apply. I'm a construction industry expert, and I've crafted this book exclusively for construction professionals.

Understand Yourself, Be a Better Leader

The way you think and act defines the way you lead. Unfortunately, most leaders don't have any concrete ways to understand their actions, and they miss out on opportunities to improve the way they think. In the leadership section, I've included an easy-to-use personal Construction Leaders Dashboard that will give you eye-opening insights into how you currently think and act. This information alone turns you into a more effective leader.

Build Better Teams, Deliver More Profitable Projects

It's challenging to put together high-performing teams that consistently turn a profit. Fortunately, there are simple ways to achieve the dream of consistent high performance. Also in the leadership section, you'll learn how to assemble and develop a team with the right people in the right roles who also understand how to achieve and maintain high performance, project after project, day after day.

Have Tough Conversations without Ruining Relationships

Whether it's with a client, a project partner, or someone from your own company, friction is inevitable in construction. The industry has a reputation for intense conflict, but the best leaders understand how to navigate disagreements and still maintain productive relationships. You'll learn how to prepare for and engage in difficult conversations that are beneficial for everyone involved.

Agree on How to Solve Problems

Ever call a meeting to solve a problem and watch as your team struggles to reach an agreement? You might think it's because they don't *want* to agree or because you're failing as a leader. This is not the case. The issue is the way your meeting is being held. I'll teach you a simple meeting structure that will lead your team to a unanimous agreement on how to solve a problem in less than thirty-seven minutes.

Eliminate Chaos

You're bombarded by project and people issues, all day, every day. You're willing to take on the challenges, but you need time away from the chaos to focus on bigger-picture items like mentoring your team and developing relationships with clients. You'll learn how to structure your calendar each week to carve out time for these essential activities.

Stop Interruptions

Have you ever reached the end of your day and wondered why you didn't accomplish your most important to-dos? I'm willing to bet that most of the time, you have an open-door policy. That means your direct reports come to you at any time with their issues and challenges. These interruptions kill your productivity and keep you from accomplishing the tasks only you can perform. You'll learn how to eliminate interruptions without abandoning your team, freeing you to complete your vital tasks.

Speak Like a Leader

To be a successful leader, you don't need charisma. You need to communicate clearly and consistently. I'll teach you three specific messages great leaders communicate to their teams, every day.

What happens when you develop your teams instead of trying to do everything yourself?

"For a recent project proposal for an internationally known, high-profile client," said Matt Buchanan, director of business development at Foushée, "Eric challenged me to engage my internal team and not just rely on myself to maximize our opportunity for landing the work. He helped me to understand that it was OK for me to take a back seat in the process and focus more on putting the right team members in the right places so that they could make the necessary presentations to be successful. You can imagine how excited I was when we did indeed land the multimillion-dollar project."

Leadership is the longest section of this chapter and of this book. As the captain steers the ship, the entire crew follows. If you are stuck micromanaging your people and building their projects, you are a leader in title and salary only. You will be unable to give your company's strategy the attention it requires. Morale will slide, marketing will falter, and sales will diminish. Profit begins and ends with the leader. So does this book.

Once you become the person your business needs you to be, then and only then are you able to shift from leader to strategist.

Step 2: The Plan: Why Strategy Second?

Strategic development means knowing your purpose, understanding and embracing your and your team's personality, writing and following a long-term plan, and keeping the number one priority the number one priority.

Good strategy varies from company to company and founder to founder. What never changes is the *result* of good strategy. *The Construction MBA* by Matt Stevens lists seven marks of effective strategy. Meaning, if you get your strategy right, you will observe these seven attributes throughout your business.

Your strategy is working when

1. you are pursuing profitable work in your niche (more on this in step 3);
2. you are building mutually beneficial, high-trust client relationships;
3. you have high confidence in your project partners;
4. your construction work is high quality and efficient;
5. you are meeting or exceeding safety standards;
6. you are being paid on time for the work you've done; and
7. you have a financial cushion to outlast lean times.

Sales and marketing may lay the foundation of a prosperous company, but good strategy excavates the land. "Fail to plan, plan to fail," the old saying goes. If you are unsure why you are doing what you are doing, your marketing team and salespeople will be, too.

Step 3: The Key: Why Sales and Marketing Last?

Sales and marketing involve knowing your niche: keeping your backlog full of the right projects for the right clients in the right locations; building relationships with the final decision maker for your current and future clients; and positioning yourself and your company for the future.

Knowing your niche in construction defies conventional wisdom. Most advice on niche-finding prioritizes the market's needs. I advise the opposite. Ask what *you* want. What projects do *you* want? What can your company deliver on time and on budget as possible? I'm not saying don't pivot to new market demand. You can and should—if it makes sense. Knowing your construction niche is a balance. It's understanding what the right project from the right client at the right location is for you . . . and pursuing those deals to the exclusion of all else.

And you need all three. For example, the right project in the wrong location with the wrong client means you lose money. A lot. Eighty percent of the time, your deals should be three for three. That occasional 20 percent will be two *for* three. Only rarely would you ever take on a one-for-three project. For example, the right client with the wrong project in the wrong location means you not only lose money but also you probably lose the relationship.

Of course, it doesn't matter your strength in finding the right client in the first place if you're pitching it to the wrong person there. It doesn't matter if you have a big backlog of projects lined up if they don't fit with what you can offer. I'll teach you how to ensure that these things don't put you out of business.

Sales and marketing are the people business of the construction industry. People do business with those they know, like, and trust. I'll tell you how to get to know the final decision makers, earn their trust, and get them to like you.

There are three things you need to do effectively to get to know people. First, get your face in the right place. Second, leave your ego at the door. Third, keep showing up.

Let me elaborate.

Construction is a long-term relationship business. When you're interacting with clients, always act as an equal. Empathize with their situation. Keep your desire to win while also accepting rejection. Be optimistic. Keep your relationships, results, and ego in balance.

There are also three practical ways construction executives can build trust: start small, be responsive, and add value.

Starting small means going for a small project first instead of a big one. Construction has a unique combination of technical difficulty, compressed timelines, risk, and cost. In a non-hard-bid environment when you're trying to establish a relationship with a new client, you're not going to walk in the door and get handed a massive job the first time you contact them. Be willing to build a small project so that you can get to know your client and develop some familiarity and comfort.

Being responsive means always answering your emails and voice mails within twenty-four hours. I get it. You've got hundreds of emails coming into your inbox at all hours, and you probably had a stressful day—or you're about to have a stressful day. But how many outstanding bid requests or client concerns do you have in your voice mail or in your email inbox, and how long have they been sitting there?

Implement the twenty-four-hour rule and respond to all emails from clients or potential clients. Be out front, proactive, and available. Your clients will appreciate that they can count on you. There is no better marketing than a real human. So be one. Answer the phone. Reply to emails. Simple acts add great value.

Adding value means positioning yourself as the trusted expert who is uniquely gifted at uncovering the problems your potential clients have. You can add value by offering them cost-saving alternatives for issues that might arise in various phases of their construction projects. Savvy owners and contractors are looking for partners who care about everyone's return on investment (ROI). Instead of throwing numbers at a bid, generate confidence in your capabilities by diving into the plans and looking for creative ways to solve problems.

Figure out what the needs of your clients are, and educate yourself to meet those needs whenever possible. If they accept your help and you're successful, you can be sure they'll like and trust you.

The bad news about this trust-building stage of construction is that sometimes you get burned. The developer talks about a sweet project, right in your wheelhouse, for five years. You spend hours and dollars on preconstruction services and then the deal never happens. The general contractor tells you you've got a shot, but they're just shopping your number. This adversity is part of the game you play. That's where your strategy reenters the field. If you know who is and is not in your niche, you can plan to invest your time only in those relationships with an excellent chance of proving fruitful. This is one of the hardest calls to make in any industry, much less construction. In the pages to come, I'll show you how.

Dan's Story, Continued

Remember Dan? Six months after I began to coach him, he was a changed man. Now in our Zoom meeting, Dan looked well rested and content. His face glowed, and the slump in his shoulders was gone.

"Eric, the best thing you taught me for time management was setting my aspirational hourly pay rate!" Dan said. "As company president, I can earn up to four hundred thousand dollars a year. That means with a forty-hour workweek, my time is worth eight hundred thirty-three dollars an hour! Now I know that every task I'm doing should be worth at least eight hundred thirty-three dollars an hour, and if it isn't, I need to delegate it or delete it.

"Before I started working with you," he continued, "I was micromanaging, doing the tasks that people who report to me were responsible for. Now my project managers run their meetings and report their results to me once a month. I block out time to develop relationships with them and help them grow as leaders. Now they're more effective interacting with clients, dealing with issues, and working with our subcontractors.

"After you taught me how to have difficult conversations, I became much more efficient in leading my people. Instead of beating around the bush and allowing an issue to go on and on, I can quickly go through the confrontation model and handle issues with skill and compassion. I can help my people understand the areas they need to improve.

"I used to be bombarded by project and people issues, all day, every day. You taught me how to set aside time away from the chaos to focus on the bigger picture. I can't thank you enough."

That's what I want you to get from this book.

Construction is the second-riskiest industry after restaurants. According to Census Bureau data, over the last ten years, construction businesses failed at nearly 1.5 times the rate of companies in other sectors. The number one reason businesses fail is cash flow, but that's just the most common symptom. In the bonus chapter of this book, you'll read a powerful case study to show you that you don't get rich in construction from growing fast. Using the proper leadership skills, you get rich from executing well.

Let's begin where I started with Dan—with getting your time back.

PART 1: CONSTRUCTION LEADERSHIP

CHAPTER 2

OWN YOUR TIME, OWN THE FUTURE

From 2004 to 2007, we were all geniuses. Anyone in construction knows what I mean. Work came easy, and the money was great. Anyone could make it in this industry.

Then we got to 2008. For the next four years, we were all idiots. Work came hard. And we had to fight for money. Reality crashed in like a wrecking ball, and many construction leaders found out the hard way that they didn't know as much as they thought they did. Businesses that couldn't adapt fast enough went under.

We all went from hero to zero. And it didn't stop there. Next came the period from 2013 to 2019. For my clients during those years, the money flowed once again. If you weren't making the big bucks, it wasn't the economy—it was you. Some thought the six-year season of plenty would never end. Again, we were all geniuses.

It seemed everything would be great forever. I'm a pessimist by nature. I'm the guy who looks at a profit and loss statement, skips the profit, and scans for the loss first.

So there I was, waiting around for something bad to happen and warning clients to prepare for the hard times. They would return. It wasn't a question of if but when, how, and why.

And then it happened. COVID-19. We all know the story. Everything changed in the blink of an eye and the tick of a watch. Unstoppable industries froze, their hundreds of billions with them. This was worse than 2008, and everybody knew it.

Despite the direst economic straits the global marketplace has ever seen, construction's cloud carried two silver linings. First, we received an exemption from the nonessential shutdowns so that we could keep building. Because civilization itself cannot survive without construction. Silver lining number two is that construction leaders are resilient. We are tough. We just kept going.

"A true man is revealed in difficult times," said Greek philosopher Epictetus. The construction industry proved its mettle when the whole world panicked and locked themselves indoors. We kept going so that the world could go on.

The unprecedented challenges of 2020, 2021, and then 2022, with the supply chain disruption, its impact on materials pricing, and broader economic downturn, taught construction leaders a critical lesson we won't soon forget—your most important resource is your time. If you have limited attention, painful distractions, a half-staffed crew, or whatever other restrictions the world throws at you, you must optimize your time. You *must*. Every building needs a foundation. As a construction leader, your foundation is your time.

Own your time or the world will own you.

Let me teach you how, beginning with a timeless management tool called the Eisenhower matrix.

The Eisenhower Matrix and the Four Ways to Spend Your Time

The following visual was first attributed to President Dwight Eisenhower and was popularized by Stephen Covey in his classic *The Seven Habits of Highly Successful People*. It's structured as a two-by-two matrix, like so:

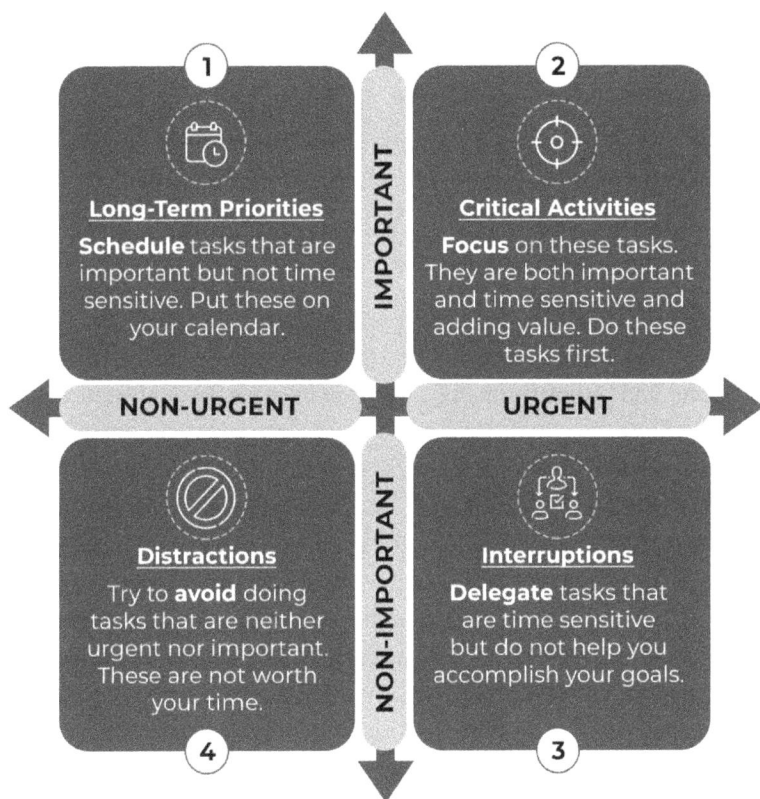

The section for long-term priorities covers tasks of high importance but low urgency. They're tasks that matter to your business that aren't pressing this week—or this very minute. Tasks that fall into the critical activities section are important and need immediate attention because they are of both high importance and high urgency. Unnecessary interruptions are of low importance and high urgency. These tasks have low importance to you personally, but other people usually see them as intensely urgent. Wasteful distractions is a category for anything of low importance and low urgency. Often, these are tasks that have no positive impact on your leadership role. Like checking email ten times per day.

The best way to leverage the matrix to get the most out of your day is to categorize how you could spend it.

Let's say you want to establish a construction branch that earns $20 million annually. That's your goal, but it's neither a vision nor a mission, which we'll talk about shortly. To achieve this goal, you'll have to shoulder several responsibilities. We might narrow these down to three specifics:

- Develop relationships and build trust with potential clients.
- Bid and land the work.
- Build profitably.

Now map these responsibilities and *all* their associated tasks onto the urgent and important matrix. For example, maybe you want to take potential clients to a basketball game. That's one way your company has chosen to develop relationships with people. But it doesn't matter if you take the client to a game next week or even next month as long as you do it at some point in the future. So this is a long-term priority because it's important but of low urgency.

Now let's say you often meet with a superintendent about the progress of a current job. Because this meeting happens on a regular basis and is necessary for the project to be profitable, it's a perfect example of a critical activity. You're also working on a bid due the following week, another critical activity of high importance and high urgency.

After we fill in the long-term priorities and the critical activities, you might tell me about the project managers who throw their problems at you all day and night. One thirty-second "I have an important question for you" after another means priorities get pushed. You can't double-book yourself. A time block is a time block for one activity at a time. (We'll talk more about blocking soon.) For now, interruptions like a project manager asking you a time-sensitive client question they should be able to handle themselves is urgent to them but of less importance to you. Not your role, not your responsibility. Unnecessary interruptions take you away from better uses of your time.

Next, we would discuss some wasteful distractions that prevent you from focusing on what is most important. Everybody has them, such as goofing around on social media. These distractions keep us from concentrating on what's of high importance and high urgency.

That's the whole project. It sounds simple, but this is a fast guide you can create to focus your time and attention, even during weeks when it feels like your world is on fire.

It should go without saying, but it does not: Your effectiveness as a leader is directly correlated with your ability to run your matrix and to successfully manage your time. You must define what's important and discipline yourself to spend approximately 80 percent of your time on long-term priorities and critical activities. This reduces the amount of time spent on unnecessary interruptions and wasteful distractions.

Easier said than done? Not with the right tools. The palm of your hand will never work on a chisel as well as a mallet will. So let's pound the right tasks into your schedule and the wrong tasks out. To both, we'll use tools as straightforward as a hammer and nails—yes and no, respectively. Say yes to what matters and no to what doesn't. Here's how.

Saying Yes to Long-Term Priorities and Critical Activities

It's not enough to want to do something. You must know why. Simon Sinek popularized this fact with his book *Start with Why*, which teaches, in short, that great leaders inspire everyone to take decisive action with a vision and a mission.

With where we're going and how we're going to get there.

With why.

So start with why.

A few paragraphs ago, I mentioned a financial goal that derives from a vision and mission, which together propel you through the hard times. They give you hope when everyone else despairs.

In my construction leadership course the Shift, I assign students the Construction Leaders Dashboard. I learned this framework from one of my mentors, Andrew Neitlich, founder of the Center for Executive Coaching. The framework starts with why—your vision and mission—but goes on to cover everything effective leaders spend their time doing. In fact, the exercise of filling out the dashboard is itself critical because doing so clarifies how you should spend your time.

The Construction Leaders Dashboard

Vision	
Mission	
Values	
Your Edge	
Initiatives (Top 3)	
Performance Metrics (Top 3)	
Key Relationships	
Development Opportunities	

Taking the time to complete the dashboard will help you release the stress that keeps many construction leaders tossing and turning at night. And it's going to help you build profit in your organization. You'll see how shortly.

The Construction Leaders Dashboard

Have you been feeling overwhelmed? Having trouble focusing on what matters most in your organization? Have you gotten complaints about your employees not being accountable or even lying? Has it been hard to stay grounded and focused on your top priorities?

If you answered yes to any of these, you need the Construction Leaders Dashboard. The dashboard not only keeps your attention on what matters most but also resolves issues of personal conflict with your organization's values and mission. And it fosters accountability in your entire company. The time you spend working on your dashboard will be like an oasis from the hurly-burly of your day-to-day life.

And I don't have to tell you—you could use *all* of that. Leading a construction company is one of the hardest challenges anyone can take on—harder even than manual labor. Before I start working with clients, they often complain that it feels impossible to get their leadership team on the same page regarding the company's direction. Performance expectations are not always clear. And you get different levels of contribution from different individuals. Leadership meetings sometimes become so tense, you get nothing done.

With the Construction Leaders Dashboard, we'll get everyone aligned, accountable, and contributing to your company's growth and success. As a result, you'll more easily attract, develop, and retain talent.

The dashboard is divided into two main sections: mindset and action. Mindset comes first. Then action. Then outcomes. Mindset is both the way you think and your fundamental, grounding philosophies of how you do business. Many people in the construction business are good at taking action, but they're misguided by the wrong mindset. If you can clarify your mindset, you'll improve the actions you take. And that results in the outcomes you're looking for. If you want to change your outcomes, change your mindset—and then choose the actions that lead to those outcomes.

With that in mind, use the form above in the following exercise to create your dashboard.

Construction Leaders Dashboard: Mindset

Your mindset has four key aspects: your vision, your mission, your values, and your edge.

Your vision is what you want your career or your business to look like over the next two to five years. What hopes and expectations do you have?

Your mission is the difference you make in both your career and your community. What contribution gets you excited about its impacts? What can your business do for your community? For your career? That's the great thing about construction: It's easy to get excited. We have an awesome impact on communities—because we build things that last and that people can use and benefit from. Think of all the families who've benefited over the years as a direct result of the work that you've done and the pay you've given your employees. You've had a massive impact on many people's lives, both in what you've built and in what you've provided. That's a lot to be proud of.

Next comes your values. What are your top three to five values, both for yourself as an individual and for your organization, that are non negotiable? These are your core values. If you haven't already, it's time to identify them.

Now what's your edge? What sets you apart from the general contractor down the street? Why would anyone want to do business with you as a subcontractor, as opposed to hundreds of other subcontractors in your area who may do the same thing? What is it that's unique about you or your organization? What attributes or strengths do you have?

Visualize it like a triangle. You have your vision and your mission at the bottom; you have your values inside at the heart; and your edge leads the way at the top. As you understand your edge, you can use it for the profitability of your business.

Now you've defined the four key aspects of your mindset as the leader in your organization. This is what you bring to the table. And this mindset is what's going to drive the actions that get you where you want to go.

Construction Leaders Dashboard: Action

Now let's talk about what your action consists of: your initiative, your performance metrics, your key relationships, and your development opportunities.

What are the most important initiatives that currently define your success? Do you know where you should focus your time, or are you scattered all over the place? Define your initiative to know where actions are best taken.

Next comes your performance metrics. How do you know when you're successful in executing your initiatives? Identify the most important performance metrics, both for your area of responsibility and for your organization, to ensure that you stay on top of how your company is doing.

How are your key relationships? At the end of the day, that's what construction is about—relationships and how you communicate within them. All things being equal in terms of technical talent and technology, it's the relationships that you build that determine your success. Who are the most critical people inside and outside your organization with whom you need to develop relationships?

Lastly comes your development opportunities. One of the reasons people are unhappy in life is because they're not growing and changing for the better. One of the great things about business is that if you want to be successful, it compels you to grow and change. So what are the experiences, assignments, and opportunities that you or people in your organization need to take advantage of in order to grow?

And remember this: Your company's growth is directly related to how much money you can make. The more you grow in your understanding of the business, the more you grow in your ability to motivate your people, the more that will impact your bottom line over time.

Saying No to Distractions and Interruptions

By this point in the chapter, you know what true construction leadership entails and why your company needs it. Saying yes to your vision and mission means saying no to any activity not aligned with your purpose.

Saying no is hard.

So let's make it easier.

Have you seen the 1978 movie *Superman*, the first one with Christopher Reeve? There's a scene in that movie with a little girl staring up into a tree where her cat is stuck. She's calling out to the cat, "Come on. Come on down from the tree!" And of course the cat's up there crying away, stuck, and not coming down. Then the film cuts away to Superman flying up in the sky and looking down. He sees the little girl crying out to the cat, and he swoops down, as Superman does, and saves the cat by taking it out of the tree. He hands the cat back to the little girl and everybody's happy.

Serious question: Why didn't the little girl ask her parents to bring a ladder to climb the tree and bring the cat down? Or if that wasn't possible, perhaps call the fire department? Was that honestly the best use of Superman's time? Shouldn't he be off saving the world and stopping murders and ending wars and protecting the innocent? As opposed to getting cats out of trees?

I call this the Superman/cat problem. It's exactly the same problem I find with many construction executives. They spend their days flying around getting cats out of trees instead of focusing on the best use of their time. So they're dealing with all these minor issues, all these small fires, and as a result they get overwhelmed and stressed out.

The simple fix is time blocks. You can use time blocks to beat the Superman/cat problem. That will reduce your stress and make you much more effective in your role.

Great Leaders Are Great Time-Blockers

If you're not familiar with the term, what I mean by a time block is a set amount of time that you spend doing only one thing. That time is blocked against any other tasks. It's also a block of time where you're focused. So time block has two meanings, and it's important to leverage them both to help focus and prevent interruptions.

As a construction executive, you may be thinking right away that this is not practical. *My days are overwhelmed by emails and phone calls and issues and project challenges. I can't shut people out!* But you can use time blocks to make you a much more effective leader.

Let me give you a quick example. When I put together an episode of my construction podcast, I use three separate ninety-minute blocks to outline and prepare the content. During the last block, I have my headphones on and listen to some Bach, because it helps me to focus. There are always multiple interruptions to that time block. Knocks on my office door. Text messages. People who want my attention. Cats who need rescuing. But I refuse to engage with those interruptions. I say no. So that I can focus on the highest and best use of my time, which is preparing the podcast episode. Otherwise, the episodes will never get out, because I'll always be rescuing cats.

You as a construction leader need to practice that same sort of discipline if you're going to be effective as a leader. And it's worth it.

Time blocks have many benefits. First, they free you up to concentrate. You do your best work when your distractions are eliminated and you can focus on what's in front of you. Think about an issue that you're facing on a project. You need to set aside time to be able to concentrate on what you're going to do to overcome that particular challenge.

The best construction executives understand that multitasking doesn't work. You must focus to achieve the best results. Yes, I realize there are times when you're doing many things at once, but if you're going to be effective, if you're going to do deep work, you have to free up time to concentrate. Because when you concentrate, it makes you more productive.

That's a natural result of concentration. You get into a flow. Ideas begin to pop, and you can overcome some of the obstacles you're facing.

Time blocks also empower you by helping your team to become more resourceful. One of the problems that you have in your leadership is that perhaps you've trained people to interrupt you constantly. Because you're always ready to solve their problems for them! The little girl knew Superman would help her because Superman rescues every cat in town. But that's a lot of cats and a lot of time spent doing things that aren't stopping murders or ending wars. Is Superman an effective leader, or is he enabling laziness?

If you discipline yourself to set aside time to work on what's most important, and if you communicate that to other people, they'll understand that at that particular point in time, they cannot interrupt you. They'll be forced to become more resourceful and solve their problems themselves.

Which means that time blocking also shows you where other people need to be trained. As you block out time to concentrate on what's most important to you and after you come out of that block, you'll begin to see where other people aren't able to perform effectively because they were waiting for some sort of input from you. They're standing there sucking their thumb like a baby instead of solving the problem. That idleness and being stuck will teach you where you need to train them.

Now let's talk honestly about the hindrance to time blocking—*you*. This relates specifically to how you perceive yourself and how that perception causes you to interact with other people. There are three core ways that you perceive yourself that hinder you from blocking out and concentrating on the highest and best use of time.

Three Behaviors That Cause Construction Leaders to Get in Their Own Way

The first is that you like being a hero. It makes you feel good when people knock on the door and interrupt you to solve their problem. You like the perception of being someone who gets stuff done. The problem with that hero mentality is it makes people dependent on you. It causes them to be passive in the way that they conduct themselves with their responsibilities. Instead of thinking that you're being the hero, you need to shift that mindset to this: "I will train others to be heroes." Then they'll be better workers and better people, and they'll stop interrupting you so that you can focus on the best use of your time and keep all your heroes happily employed.

The second hindrance is perfectionism. One of the reasons why you are in your position as a construction leader is because you are highly competent. You're good at what you do. But what I found working with many construction executives over the years is that they are perfectionists, and the source of that perfectionism is their pride. The problem with that is it takes power and responsibility away from others. Perfectionism leads you to believe that only you can do a particular task. And if anyone else does it, they won't do it quite as well as you can. So you continue to do things that other people should be doing, which causes you to get stuck. The fix for this is that you need to be content with good enough. That doesn't mean you're sloppy or you're careless, but you must be satisfied with other people executing tasks in a manner that is good enough for the particular circumstance, or for the project, or for the client. You need to focus on delegating those tasks that you tend to hold on to because of your perfectionism. Release them to other people. Good enough is good enough. Train those other people to perform at a good enough level, even if they can't reach your level of performance.

The third hindrance to time blocking is the nice-guy syndrome, the source of which is fear. Some leaders like to be perceived as a nice person. The problem with this is it gives people permission to constantly interrupt you. And poor planning on their part begins to constitute an emergency on your part. The way you fix that is by learning to say no. As a construction leader, you need to get good at saying no to people when they request time from you if that request is going to interrupt your ability to concentrate on what's most important. It's more critical for you to be respected and effective than to be liked, and you must make that shift. Practice saying no so that others stop interrupting you. Don't allow yourself to be dependent on people liking you. Be confident enough in your abilities and in the way that you perform to be content with people respecting you so that you can be as effective as possible.

Three Types of Time Blocks

Let's talk about the types of blocks you can employ as a construction leader. The first is a project block, in which you set aside a certain amount of time to focus on a particular project. Whether you have an estimating issue, or you're a project manager, or you're a superintendent, you set aside a block of sixty to ninety minutes to work on a specific project. I find this is particularly true for estimators; they need to set aside time to focus on a takeoff or to zero in on the quantities. That helps you get your arms around the project and deliver an estimate that is going to set up the organization for building a profitable project.

The second time block is a people block. One reason why construction leaders get overwhelmed is because they have too many people reporting to them. The first thing you want to do is restructure your organization so that you have no more than four to six people reporting to you. After that, one way to make your time usage more effective is to block out an hour to meet with each one of your direct reports every week. This will help you eliminate the number of times they approach you with issues throughout the week, because they'll know they have a standing appointment with you every week to spend time face-to-face discussing the issues and challenges they have. Blocking out time to meet with your people on a regular basis will help to eliminate some of the distractions and the overwhelm.

The last block is a geographic block. Most construction leaders spend a lot of time on the road. I call it windshield time. For many, this is wasted time because they do not block their time effectively in terms of where they are geographically. Thus, they may visit one job site in Sacramento, California, then another down in San Jose, in the South Bay Area, and perhaps they've got another job in the Central Valley. They visit the first job site at seven o'clock in the morning and then spend two or three hours on the road driving down to San Jose and then another two hours getting over to the Central Valley. It's a waste of time. They spent half their week on the road instead of planning what sites to visit and when so that they cut down on windshield time. When you're planning to visit multiple sites, think about how you can block out your time geographically so that you're much more effective and focused. Narrow down your windshield time.

Now you may be reading this and saying to yourself, *Eric, this is completely unrealistic. You don't understand my life. Multitasking is essential.* Believe me, I do understand where you're coming from. But I'd like you to just reflect for a minute. Whether you realize it or not, you are already employing time blocks in your life. In fact, you spend a third of your time focused on a time block: sleeping. How many other things are you doing while you're sleeping? I hope the answer is zero. I know it sounds a little silly, but when you're sleeping, you're not multitasking. You're sleeping! You're not doing anything else. So if you sleep somewhere between six and eight hours a night, which, by the way, will help your effectiveness, you are already blocking out time for something that's important.

I understand that sleep is a physical necessity. And some of your other tasks don't feel as important. But blocking out time to focus on things that are most important is an absolute necessity if you're going to be an effective leader. A client I worked with some time ago was transitioning from a project manager into a general manager role, and he was feeling a lot of overwhelm, particularly as he was wrapping up one project that he was responsible for and moving into more general manager-type responsibilities. At my urging he decided to block out his afternoons to focus on finishing that project and then leave his mornings open for questions and issues from the people who reported to him. In other words, in the morning he was open to interruptions. He was open to fire drills. But in the afternoon, he was going to be focused. His people got used to that schedule, and it cut down on his interruptions during his blocked time.

Then he broke up his focused time. He spent twenty-five minutes working on a particular issue or a challenge. Then he took a five-minute break before jumping onto the next issue. He repeated that four times. Twenty-five minutes on, five minutes off, repeated four times. After he finished that, he took a thirty-minute break to do something else. Perhaps he took a walk or answered emails. He used those blocks of time to focus on the challenges and the issues that he needed to concentrate on in order to be the most effective leader.

Just Say No

To make time blocking work, you must be able to say no.

Let me qualify this a little: It doesn't mean you spend your whole day saying, "No, no, no, no, no." What you want to do is notice where the interruptions are coming from and from whom. To do this, you need to understand the difference between distractions and interruptions.

I'll let the cat out of the bag and spoil this for you: The distractions come from you. Right? It's always our choice. The distractions come from hitting the crack pipe, meaning the thing we have that gives us dopamine hits. We've all got the crack pipe, whether it's a favorite phone game or text messages or social media. You get distracted hitting the crack pipe for whatever reason, usually to reduce stress or to give yourself a boost.

But the interruptions come from others, and we allow them. The interruptions come because you haven't trained people to work without you or you haven't delegated or you haven't held them accountable for doing their job. You're allowing them to interrupt you. Really, they're asking you to do their job for them, but they're doing that because you've trained them to ask you.

Learn to say no to interruptions. As you do so, make a note of where the interruptions are coming from, because that tells you where you need to train, where you need to delegate, and where you need to hold people accountable.

Close your door to show that you mean it. You will still meet with your people, but what you will say to them is this: "No, I'm not going to handle this now, but I will meet with you first thing tomorrow and we'll talk about it," or "I'll meet with you in an hour after I finish this task."

The fact that you're at where you are in life tells us both that you already have enough self-discipline to prevent the distractions from getting you. It's the interruptions that are killing you, whether these are tasks, time-wasters, or even people.

Speaking of people, who is your biggest interrupter? Write that person's name down. Then write down what you can do in the next thirty days to solve that constant interruption problem. If it's your boss, then you need to talk to them about that. Perhaps you need to say, "Hey, boss. Would it be possible for us to block out time for this discussion?" I'm not saying blow your boss off. What I am saying is discuss how to schedule this more effectively so that you're not interrupted all the time. That's still saying no to your boss, but it's saying no for a purpose.

Say no, explain why, then provide an alternative. And make a plan to solve the interruption problem so that you don't spend your whole block of time saying no to everyone.

Time Management Activities and Exercises

Your time is your best resource. You know this well now. How you spend your time determines how your business goes. You know this, too. There are high-return activities and low-return activities. To say yes to the urgent and essential is to say no to the optional and trivial—and vice versa. Scheduling blocks of time throughout your day and your week ensures that you do what needs to get done.

But is there more? Are there other ways and means to extract maximum value from your most precious resource? You can probably tell I'm asking rhetorically because, of course, there are.

Time blocking and leveraging the power of no are the concrete and steel of building a high-performance schedule. As with every construction job, though, you need more. Electrical. Mechanical. Windows and doors. Paint. Get as granular as you like with the materials of a typical construction job, and you'll reach my point. I'd like you to get everything you can out of every minute of your day. Not just the days and the hours. *The minutes.*

Execution at the minute level separates the good from the great—the guy who got lucky from true genius with resilience to outlast multiple recessions.

In the Shift, I give students two additional time management exercises—the time inquiry and the log. Together, these tools empower you to micromanage your time and not your people.

The Time Inquiry

The time inquiry exercise is another tool I got from Andrew Neitlich. Credit where it's due.

This practice will help you focus on where you can spend your time to achieve your desired results. The questions may feel harsh, but answering them will help you be honest with yourself, which in turn will help you spend your time wisely. Write down your answers to the following:

1. What are your biggest issues with time management?
2. What are the costs to you professionally and personally because of how you are spending your time now?
3. What are the opportunity costs of how you spend your time—things that you could be doing but you can't because of your current use of time?
4. What are examples of where you are spending time on things that don't have high strategic value or importance?
5. What are examples of where you are spending time that others could do instead?
6. What are examples of where you are doing things more perfectly than they need to be done?
7. How can you express your time management issue as a clear goal? For instance, in terms of the number of hours worked per week or how you change the percentage of time you spend on key issues.
8. What would your ideal day look like in terms of the number of hours and how you spend that time?
9. What beliefs do you have about setting boundaries or asserting or giving up control that might be at play?
10. What else comes up for you about managing your time?

The Time Log

It's time to keep track of your day. Map out how you spend your time by breaking down each day into fifteen-minute increments starting at 5:00 a.m. and stopping at 7:45 p.m. Then write down what you do after 7:45 p.m. in a general note. Yes, this sounds like a lot of micromanagement and will probably take several pages. But you need to know how you spend your time.

Keep this log for two weeks. At the end of each day, grade yourself, from A to F, on how well you used your time. Then note your best day and your worst day over the two weeks and why they were different.

Own Your Time

When you control the use of your time, you control your results. There's no better way to boost your productivity and that of your entire organization. You are the role model for everyone.

But if you don't control your time, you'll always be at the mercy of your environment. You can live that way during the good years, but the hard times will gut your business and ruin your life. You've got to control your time so that you stay strong when the next catastrophe outside your control strikes.

Because it will.

Time management isn't the only factor that will lead to success. High-performing teams will also help you meet your goals, and we'll discuss that next.

CHAPTER 3

PREPARING FOR HIGH PERFORMANCE

Everyone wants a high-performing team. But if you were to ask each team member what that means, their answers will probably be all over the place. "We do our jobs really well? We come out ahead on projects? We work hard?"

Vague answers, vague outcomes. If we don't have measurable behaviors to foster or precise goals to hit, we're cutting without a guide. That's no way to achieve a big dream. To make it happen, we've got to use clear measurements—and shared definitions. That's what this chapter is all about.

How to Measure High Performance

What is high performance in the first place? Let's agree on a definition—concentrating on the few tasks that, if done with excellence, will impact your job performance and your company's results. It means that a few tasks done right make the rest of the work go better.

This might seem fairly obvious, now that we've got a definition on paper. A better way, I've found, to define a person, place, or thing is by what it's not. So to grasp the depth of high performance in this great industry of ours, let's have a look at its opposite—low performance.

Low Performers versus High Performers

There's a great book called *The Mental Game of Baseball* by Harvey Dorfman. Even if you don't like baseball, you'll find it instructive. It covers the many differences between low performers and high performers.

Low performers have a goal.

High performers have a process.

That doesn't mean you shouldn't set goals, but you need to have a process to help you achieve each goal.

Low performers stop when they achieve something.

High performers understand that the initial achievement is just the beginning.

Low performers think they're good at everything.

High performers understand their circles of competence, their edge.

One of your jobs is to help your team members identify their edges and make sure they're exploiting them as much as possible.

Low performers take feedback and coaching as personal criticism.

High performers know they have weak spots and seek out thoughtful critiques.

Low performers value isolated performance.

High performers value consistency.

Some folks crush it on project A but not on project B. I'd rather have someone I can trust to bring the project in profitably every time.

Low performers give up at the first sign of trouble and assume they're failures.

High performers see failure as a part of the path to growth and mastery.

We've all experienced failure in our careers. That means the people who report to you will fail. But as long as they're not repeating the same mistakes, they're on the path to growth. We shouldn't beat ourselves up if we're making progress.

Low performers have no clue what improves the odds of achieving good outcomes. You ask them, "Why were you profitable on that project?"

"I don't know. I guess we just got lucky."

High performers understand what they need to do to bring a project in on time, under budget, and safely.

Low performers show up to practice to have fun. High performers realize that what happens in practice happens in games.

Let's say you're on the way to a job handoff meeting between estimating and the project management. This meeting is essential to the project's outcome, so you've got to go in with intensity.

Low performers focus on identifying their weaknesses and improving them. High performers focus on their strengths and find people who are strong where they are weak. This is true for senior leadership in particular.

Stop trying to improve your weaknesses. Start finding people who are strong in the areas where you're weak and get them going. I am weak at video editing, so I send video to a guy who will get it done in less than two hours.

Focusing on being right is low performance. Focusing on getting the best outcome is high performance.

Low performers think knowledge is power.

High performers pass on wisdom and advice.

Some people in senior leadership do not share their wisdom with people underneath them because they are afraid they'll steal their jobs. Ballers ball. And if you're a baller, there's room for you in construction. Share your wisdom and advice!

Low performers think good outcomes always result from their brilliance. High performers understand what outcomes result from luck. Sometimes you do get lucky.

Low performers focus on tearing others down.

High performers focus on making everyone better.

Low performers make decisions in committees so that no one person is responsible if things go wrong. High performers make decisions as individuals. That doesn't mean they don't get feedback from people, but they make decisions and take responsibility for those decisions.

Blaming others is low performance. Accepting responsibility is high performance.

Low performers show up inconsistently.

High performers show up every day.

Do what the high performers do. Model that behavior for others, and teach them the expectations of high performance.

Yeah, OK, but that's easy for you to say, you might be thinking. *Don't just tell me, "High performance is easy, so just do it."*

If that's on your mind, you'd be right. One hundred percent right. Peak performance is easy—when everything lines up perfectly. But that seldom happens in a complex process like a construction job. There are too many variables. Projects involve managers, subcontractors, suppliers, and many more people. There's only so much over which you have control. Despite it all, you want everyone to work at a high level. So how do you perform in pressure situations, particularly when things don't go your way?

Achieving the Right Outcomes

Start by categorizing each moving part by whether you have total control, some control, or no control. Then focus on doing what you have total control over to the best of your ability. That way, you maximize your chances of achieving the outcomes you're looking for.

"What outcomes?" you might ask. "Aren't you just trying to finish a job?"

No. You're trying to accomplish multiple outcomes with each job. I'll give you an example. What outcomes is a project manager responsible for? Of course they must complete the project. But they also must do it on time, safely, within budget, and ensure its quality as it's completed. It's more complicated than it sounds.

What are the top three outcomes you're expected to achieve in your position?

Here's an example. I have a client I'll call Mike, who is in charge of quality control in the fabrication shop. Mike identified three outcomes that were most important to his job: doing quality work, teaching fitters and welders building codes, and having inspectors on-site as needed.

Let's start with your single most important outcome. Which of your top three is the most important? Mike chose doing quality work as his top outcome.

Next, I had Mike pick the top three tasks that produce that outcome. He came up with accurate measurements, attention to detail, and spreading knowledge to those who work for him.

In order to achieve *your* number one outcome, what are the top three tasks you need to focus on?

I then asked Mike, "What is the most important task that leads to your most important outcome?" Mike chose accurate measurements. Everything else depended on getting that right.

Pick the most important task that leads to your most important outcome. In what specific ways can you improve your performance of that task?

I asked Mike, "In what specific ways can you improve your performance in taking accurate measurements?"

Mike took two minutes to write down all the ideas he could come up with. The first was to take the time to understand what he's measuring. Number two was to establish running dimensions. The third was to ensure his equipment was up to par.

I asked him to pick the most important of those ideas, and he chose the third one—his equipment. Then we brainstormed ways he could keep on top of that task to ace it every time.

Mike started out wanting to achieve high performance. By breaking his job into tiny parts, he realized the best approach was to focus on ensuring his equipment was good so that he could get accurate measurements that would result in high-quality work.

Grab a pen and think through the same approach in your position.

1. What are the top three outcomes you're expected to achieve in your position?
2. Which of those outcomes is the most important?
3. What three tasks can you focus on to best achieve that outcome?

4. Which of those tasks is the most important to achieving that outcome?
5. In what specific ways can you improve your performance on that task?
6. Which way is most important to improving that task?

Choose the most important thing you can do to improve performance on your most important task that leads to your most important outcome. *This* is what matters for high performance—driving it and ensuring that you're getting important things done.

Once you have these answers, you can build an action plan to succeed at that task 100 percent of the time. You've now done most of the work to reach high-performing status. After you've mastered one task, go back and follow the same process for the other tasks. Then go back and follow it all the way through for your other two outcomes. But be sure that you focus only on *one* task at a time.

Breaking down your outcomes into tasks like this provides your individual performance metrics. It shifts your focus to practical, concrete steps that improve your performance at the task that leads to your most important outcome. (I'll show you a powerful tool to do this in the next chapter).

TDAAT: The Five Areas of High Performance

There are five areas that influence achieving high performance:

- Technique: mastering skills
- Discipline: mastering habits
- Attitude: a positive mindset
- Association: who you hang out with
- Time: giving yourself time to improve

You can remember them by the acronym TDAAT.

Let me tell you a story about a girl named Mary. When she was thirteen years old, Mary decided to break the world record in the two-hundred-meter butterfly. She was a good swimmer at that time. But the one thing she didn't do to go for that goal was swim more. Instead, she made two qualitative changes.

First, she made a commitment to show up on time for practice. Swimmers get started at the same time that construction folks do, at 4:00 a.m. Second, she began touching with two hands at the end of her laps to get faster.

In 1979, at the age of fourteen, Mary Meagher broke the world record in the butterfly swim. And in 1984, at the Los Angeles Olympics, she won three gold medals. She said of her victories, "People don't know how ordinary success is."

What about you? Think back to a time when you succeeded in academics, sports, or your career. What changes did you make?

The key performance-affecting areas are technique, discipline, attitude, association, and time. You needn't change all five. Just pick a couple. Mary made a qualitative change. You may need to make a quantitative change. That's fine.

When I was a high school senior, I was failing biology—a class I had to pass to graduate. So I made discipline, attitude, and time changes. I studied for the last test because I had to get an A. I did, and I graduated. It all came down to TDAAT.

Think about your current role. What is one change you can make in technique, discipline, attitude, association, or time that will allow you to perform at a higher level? This can help your team focus on how they can improve their performance.

Four Traits of a High-Performing Team

Now that we've defined high performance and discussed how to measure it—specific outcomes and areas of influence—let's now look at the high-performance mindset. If greatness from every member of your team is the output, these traits are the input.

I'll describe each one of these traits and discuss how you can promote them in your company to get the best out of everyone—without burning anyone out.

Hunger

Hunger is a desire born from a lack—whether physical, mental, or social.

Think of a food you enjoy that you haven't had for a long time. You may want to go right out and eat it now!

Hunger is a powerful motivator. Ask yourself and others in your construction company, "What is the hunger that drives you?" Hunger focuses your energy, and it encourages you to be creative with resources. You need to know who's hungry and for what. Your company's hunger to be excellent, to succeed, or to get the next project will keep you motivated.

How is hunger expressed practically? If you're hungry, you'll dedicate your efforts to satiating that hunger. And you'll persist in that effort until you're satisfied.

Hunger also leads to ingenuity. If you're hungry for something, you're going to figure out how to satiate that desire. If you hunger to build a successful company, if your team craves completing valuable projects, you will take the initiative. You will be ingenious and dedicate yourself to fulfilling that hunger.

What motivates sports teams? Winning is an obvious motive. So is the recognition that comes from winning.

Money is another big motivator. So is the sense of accomplishment, even on a team. Having a sense of family motivates a lot of people. They love being on teams because there's a feeling of belonging and camaraderie.

Successful companies are like sports teams in that they're hungry for wins and recognition. Of course they want to make money. But they also want to have a sense of pride and accomplishment. The greatest companies have that feeling of family that characterizes the best sports teams.

A motivator that goes hand in hand with the hunger to win is the desire for mastery. If you're going to play at the highest level, you have to master your craft.

Hard Work

The second trait of a successful team is hard work. It's one thing to be hungry. It's another to put in the work to satiate that hunger. Because hunger is universal, but hard work is not.

To paraphrase a proverb of King Solomon, "No matter how much you want something, laziness won't help a bit. But hard work will reward you with more than enough."

We're not just talking about any hard work but *intelligent* hard work. Work harder, work smarter.

As a leader, people are always looking to you for an example. If you're not demonstrating hunger and hard work yourself, your people won't embrace those traits.

So how do you work hard and smart in construction?

First, you have to understand the job with clarity. You have to gain technical competence at the project you're building from a bidding, planning, and building standpoint.

Second, you have to look at the project from your customer's perspective. Because you are providing products and services in exchange for money, it behooves you to put yourself in your customers' shoes. That means asking what they want out of the project. What are their requirements? What constitutes a good experience for them?

It's not always easy to look at a project from your customer's perspective. But if you can, you'll receive insights that help you meet the customer's needs.

Third, you must look at each project from your company's perspective. This is particularly important for positions like project manager, estimator, and superintendent. How does it fit into the organization's overall strategy? Where does it fit in relation to other projects? How will resources be allocated?

Sometimes not every construction project gets the same level of attention and resources. It can be discouraging when you're on a lower-priority project. But it's your job to understand how it fits into the big picture. As a result, you can be content and focus on how to execute.

It's also important for the organization's leaders to communicate where each project fits. They must assure their people that when leadership is not lavishing attention on a job, it is not a judgment against them. Leaders also need to know that having fewer resources can impede performance.

Fourth, you have to communicate. I just met with a client who brought their estimators, project managers, project engineers, superintendents, and foremen into the room. We discussed how they could all work together more effectively. Everyone called for better communication across the company's divisions. You will have to optimize communication if you want to be a successful construction company.

Fifth, you must be competent.

What's harder, firefighting or fire prevention? I'm no expert, but I would guess firefighting is more taxing. In construction, we tend to spend a lot of time firefighting and not enough time on fire prevention. The reason is often a lack of competence. And the result is a lot of extra hard work.

A couple of years ago, I was helping a young construction professional in dispatch figure out how to improve her job performance. After thinking about the outcomes she needed to achieve and the tasks that led to those outcomes, she committed to spending thirty minutes a day chatting with her foreman. That way, she'd be sure they'd communicated everyone's needs clearly.

I asked her what the impact of that proactivity would be. She said it would help to reduce her stress in a major way. She committed to that upfront work to prevent the fires that often occur from lack of communication.

Make sure your team is doing all the hard work needed to succeed. Because if you're hungry and you're working hard, you're halfway to the highest performance possible.

Humility

By humility, I mean the opposite of vanity. It's an appropriate view of yourself with honesty about your limitations. It's neither tearing yourself down nor puffing yourself up.

It's the worst athletes who say, "There's nothing I can do to improve." We hate those guys. And they usually slide into terrible behaviors after proclaiming their own greatness.

That's not to say the best guys lack confidence. They have a great deal of confidence, which is sometimes misinterpreted as arrogance. But they're always working on their craft. They seek out coaches to teach them the next step.

Like the top athletes, the best construction executives never feel they've arrived. They've always got something to learn.

Why is humility important? Because life is full of ups and downs. The ups may be of your doing, but they may not. When things are going well, you can get a sense of entitlement and complacency. Many construction entrepreneurs once thought nothing could ever go wrong. Then 2008 happened.

You might have the hunger. Maybe you've put in the hard work. But you're still experiencing failure. That can be discouraging.

Humility is also important because you don't want to rise too high during the ups. And when you're down, you don't want to get too low. People with true humility keep an even keel.

Let's talk about how you can live with humility in your company.

Number one, show up every day and put in the work. Humility starts with not feeling too important to take on the tasks that need doing.

Number two, commit to supporting other people. If you're too much of a big shot to support someone, you're not a leader. You're an arrogant loser who's about to crash when your people bail out. Give support to those who need it—especially your team, who rely on you to be their leader.

Number three, squash your selfishness. It's not all about you. You're there to support others; construction is a team sport. If you want to take it all for yourself and leave nothing for everyone else, you'll soon be a team of one. Don't eat the best meals alone. Feed the people sitting at your table.

My favorite football team, the San Francisco 49ers, had a memorable 2019 season before losing the Super Bowl to the Kansas City Chiefs. During their NFC championship win, Jimmy Garoppolo, their quarterback, threw the ball only eight times during the penultimate game of the Niners' season. Afterward, reporters kept asking him some variation of "Jimmy, don't you wish you would have thrown it more?"

But Jimmy said, in effect, "No, because the Niners were running the ball so well."

He didn't have to make it all about him. He was just interested in winning. That's a real expression of humility. If you have to be the one who looks the best, you're not leading and you're not humble. You're hogging the spotlight.

Number four, admit mistakes quickly. How long does it take you to admit you blew it and apologize? It hurts, but it needs to be said. The longer it takes, the more the pain will increase. When you make a mistake, admit it as soon as possible. Your team will spend less time being frustrated with you and more time making up lost ground.

Number five, take responsibility while you spread the credit. One of my clients got an award for a headline-grabbing project they built in the Bay Area. When the award was announced, company executives brought the project manager and his young project engineer onstage, too. They stood up there as a team and shared the credit together.

The executives could have taken the award themselves and kept the guys in the field out of it. They didn't. They shared the spotlight. This is testimony to their senior management. And it's a real example of what it means to be humble, as a leader in particular. Don't try to garner all the praise for yourself. Be willing to share it with your people.

Happiness

We've discussed being hungry, working hard, and having humility. Now let's talk about being happy. Because if you hate your job, you won't perform with excellence. Effective, strong teams are happy teams.

Happiness is a pervasive feeling of well-being, joy, and contentment. It isn't due to external factors; instead, it's something we can cultivate in our lives.

What does it mean to be content? It means to be accepting of the situation you're in. If you're content, you resist losing your mind over adverse situations because you're aware of the good you retain. You can also be content when things are going well.

Again, you don't get too high. And when things are going badly, you don't get too low. You're just OK with a circumstance that you're in.

The opposite of contentment is unhappiness. How is unhappiness manifested? Complaints, grumbling, and self-pity. What makes us unhappy? One of the major reasons people aren't happy is they aren't good at anything.

Think about the excellence of professional sports teams. We spend a lot of time watching other people be excellent. Yet we don't take the time to cultivate excellence in our vocations, our hobbies, or our relationships. As a result, we struggle with the things that mean the most to us. And it causes a great deal of unhappiness.

Another reason why people aren't happy is they do things they know are wrong or they don't do things they know are right. People don't put enough effort into maintaining good relationships with those who are most important to them at work and at home.

Doing wrong instead of right and not putting in effort where you should are big problems. They're the core of a bad life experience. But you don't leave your misery at home. That kind of unhappiness bleeds into the work you do. So you need to be happy to perform at a high level.

How can you cultivate happiness on a regular basis? You need to get small wins under your belt. One way to do that is committing to communication in your business and embracing the construction process every day.

One of my clients said to me recently, "Construction sucks, but it's fun." You could also say, "Life sucks, but it's fun."

You've got to embrace that attitude and pay attention to the process. Understand that one day doesn't sum up your whole life, and one week doesn't sum up the success of a project. You can take incremental steps to getting wins day by day, week by week, and month by month.

If you combine hard work, hunger, and humility, you will be a happy person who can rack up wins and build thriving teams. All four traits are essential to high performance.

Being hungry but not working hard makes you unhappy. You'll just starve. If you're hungry and work hard but you lack humility, not only will you never be happy but also you will never create a happy team. There'll always be something missing.

If you were to ask anyone on your team how they define high performance, the last thing they'll tell you is this: "High performance is where something is missing."

Hunger, hard work, humility, happiness. Cultivate them all.

How? That's an excellent question.

I want you to think about the people in your organization. Are they hungry?

If there's any hesitation at all, let me offer you this tip.

One way to develop hunger within your organization is to set goals—for the company or for the projects—that stretch folks but are attainable. Then set an example by diligently pursuing those goals. That's where the dedication to hard work comes back in.

I encourage teams to do what many consider the hardest work of all: holding each other accountable. Don't make assumptions about people and situations. Find out the truth. Communicate up and down the chain of command.

Executives should keep their doors open to people in the field. And folks in the field should communicate up and down the chain of command. They've got to look beyond their projects to see the bigger picture.

As a leader, you should lead by example. Always be asking yourself, "How can I get better?"

Don't be content with where you are. Look at how to fill your skill gaps in areas that build the most humility. Make sure you are spreading the credit and recognizing people in your organization publicly and privately.

Being happy is simple. Stop doing what you shouldn't be doing, whatever that might be. Start doing what you know you should. And while you're at it, resist the temptation to complain if things aren't perfect. Things are never perfect. Have the important conversations with your people, and be content with making incremental progress toward executing projects in the most profitable ways.

The Action of High Performance

We've talked about evaluating your team, the mindset of high performers, and TDAAT. Now let's look at the action of high performance.

Madison Bumgarner has made three World Series appearances for the San Francisco Giants and was the MVP of one. In game seven of the 2014 World Series against the Kansas City Royals, he came in to pitch in the fifth inning with the Giants clinging to a one-run lead.

Think about the environment he walked into. He stood on the mound, surrounded by fifty thousand people wearing Kansas City Royals blue. All those people hoped he'd fail at his job. Talk about pressure!

So what did he focus on in that situation? He focused on his actions, throwing hard strikes.

In the bottom of the ninth, with two outs, the Giants were still clinging to the one-run lead. The batter got up and hit a looping line drive to left center field. If you're a Giants fan, you can still picture it.

The center fielder, Gregor Blanco, came running in on the looping line drive. He faced a choice: Make a diving catch, get the last out, and be a hero. Or field the ball on the bounce, keep it to a single, and get it back in. Blanco did neither. The ball bounced all the way back to the fence.

Then the left fielder, Juan Perez, came up and kicked the ball, playing Little League in the World Series. So the hitter got all the way to third base on what should've been a single.

The pressure grew even worse. If you were Madison Bumgarner, having pitched your heart out for four innings, what would you do at that point?

You'd do what anyone should when a job is on the line and you've got to get results. You'd concentrate on the few tasks that, if done with excellence, would make a difference in the results.

In the bottom of the ninth with two outs and a guy on third, you have two choices: You can fall apart and blame someone else, or you can focus on the tasks you can control. That means you throw hard strikes. That's what Bumgarner did. And the next batter ended up fouling out to Pablo Sandoval.

Madison Bumgarner helped the Giants win their third World Series in five years by focusing on the tasks he could control when the pressure was on.

High performance doesn't just happen. You've got to drive it with metrics, accountability, consistency, the right mindset, and constant communication. If you follow through on these steps, your team will perform better than you ever dreamed.

So how do you follow through? I'll show you in the next chapter.

CHAPTER 4

BUILDING AND LEADING A HIGH-PERFORMING TEAM

High performance is definable and manageable. By now you know this well.

In the previous chapter, we discussed what are, in essence, the soft skills of a high-performing team. You're able to categorize what you do and don't have control over, for example. Your people can, on their own, figure out the top three outcomes they're responsible for. And they (and you) are together nurturing the traits that lend themselves to high performance.

In my garage, I have an orange toolbox my late friend Stan gave me. He was a great guy who immigrated from Ireland to the United States, worked hard, and built a mini real estate empire that included an apartment building. Stan did most of the maintenance work himself. He gave me the toolbox as a gift—and as a hint to fix up some stuff around my house.

Stan gave me that toolbox years ago. Now I'm going to give you a tool: the Ninety-Day High-Performance Dashboard. It's my go-to tool for building high performance into construction organizations as small as a few employees on up to billions in annual revenue. As with leadership, high performance demands a dashboard.

The Ninety-Day High-Performance Dashboard

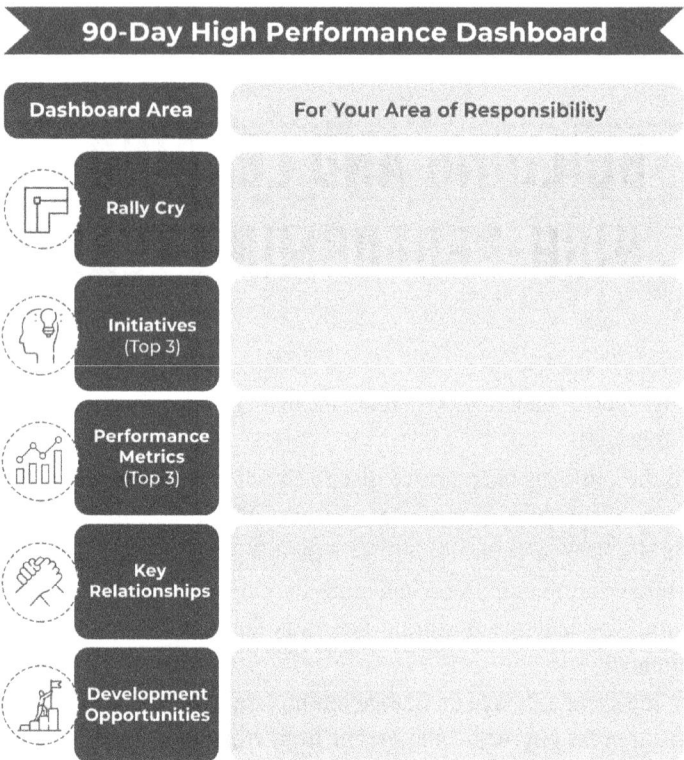

90-Day High Performance Dashboard	
Dashboard Area	**For Your Area of Responsibility**
Rally Cry	
Initiatives (Top 3)	
Performance Metrics (Top 3)	
Key Relationships	
Development Opportunities	

This dashboard, an adaptation of the Construction Leaders Dashboard, is designed to help the people who report to you directly to think about how to achieve high performance, act accordingly, and troubleshoot their behavior as needed. That will help you maximize their productivity and make your leadership job easy.

When used correctly, this tool will enable you to hold your direct reports accountable for their performance while strengthening your relationship.

Who Is This Tool For?

If you're a project executive, you have project managers reporting directly to you. If you lead an estimating group, you have estimators reporting to you. If you're a superintendent, you have foremen reporting to you. And if you're the chief executive or the president, you have all those types of folks reporting to you.

Are you satisfied with their performance at the moment? Do you find yourself doing their jobs for them? Are they not making the progress in their careers that you'd like them to make?

If you answered yes, this tool can help you. Because your people's performance reflects the quality of your leadership. Great leaders help folks overcome their tendencies to be overwhelmed, selfish, or fearful—all of which can keep people from doing their best.

You have a duty to help your direct reports do their best. They're not cogs in the machine. They're human beings. And those human beings help determine your profitability. If you do a good job of developing them, they will ensure the future strength of your organization.

Use this dashboard whenever you bring on a new hire or promote someone. This tool can even be useful when demoting or shifting someone to another position.

It's a common meme that meetings are a waste of time. I disagree. The only meetings that waste time are poorly run meetings.

All business is based on the strength of interpersonal relationships. That goes double for construction. Here, meetings are opportunities to build those relationships and to positively influence the people who report to you. So it's essential that you have regular one-on-one meetings with your direct reports.

You can base the content of those one-on-one meetings on this dashboard. It can help you build accountability and help your direct reports stay on track in terms of their performance.

How Does the Dashboard Help?

You'll want to foster two key experiences in your team meetings—clarity and accountability.

Clarity

Many people lack clarity about what they need to achieve. They have tons of demands coming at them from different angles, which makes it hard for them to prioritize. They don't block out time to focus on high-priority items. As a result, they never get things done.

The dashboard is designed to help give folks clarity on what's most important. And with that clarity comes focus.

Walk around your office, and you may see your direct reports working, but they're not as focused as they could be. It's not that they're lazy. Most of them are just distracted by too many demands.

The dashboard can help your people focus on their daily tasks, cultivate necessary relationships, and develop opportunities to grow. They can get focused on executing the initiatives they need to reach excellence.

When your team gets focused, they can progress in development and executing what maximizes your organization's profitability. This dashboard will open up opportunities for accountability conversations that deepen relationships, grow productivity, and foster excellence.

Accountability

Make accountability an integral part of your culture.

Accountability need not be difficult if it's consistent. Nor does it have to be uncomfortable. As a leader, you should always be asking, "Did you do what you said you were going to do? What challenges are you facing that I can help you with?"

Measurable parameters make accountability easier. If you use this tool consistently, it will facilitate your role as a leader. Because it will keep you from doing other people's jobs for them.

Getting lost in the weeds is a result of unclear parameters and a lack of focus, clarity, and urgency to perform. Fixing these issues will help make your projects more profitable because the full breadth of your workforce will be engaged in those projects at a high level. And that will give you more time for strategic thinking. Consistent accountability might even help you get home earlier to spend time with your family.

The dashboard is designed with consistency in mind. It will help you communicate how people across your organization should execute at a high level. It also gives you and your direct reports a shared vocabulary to increase your conversations' effectiveness and deepen their impact.

Why Ninety Days?

Ninety days is a good chunk of time to get stuff done. It's not long enough to lose your urgency, but it's not so short that you get overwhelmed.

Several years ago, I spoke with Jeff Hoopes, the CEO of Swinerton, about a project I was developing. At the end of our discussion, Jeff told me, "You should do a podcast on these subjects that you're exploring."

I put together a simple ninety-day plan to launch my podcast, *Construction Genius*. Three months later, it was up and running. That wasn't an easy lift for me, but it was doable. Not only was I able to build up the podcast's back end but also I secured a number of interviews before launch.

That's why you should use ninety-day plans with your direct reports. It keeps them moving forward, focuses them on incremental improvement, and gives them what I call patient impatience.

You have to be patient in terms of progress, but you must always be moving forward. Ninety days is the perfect amount of time to preserve that balance.

How Do You Use This Tool?

The Ninety-Day High-Performance Dashboard consists of five aspects. I'll go through it step-by-step so that you understand each one. Then you'll be able to share the dashboard with the people in your organization.

1. Rally Cry

If you woke up at three thirty in the morning to get to a job site and were asked why, could you provide a clear answer? And could you motivate someone else to work just as hard toward the same goal? You could with the right rally cry.

A rally cry is a clear statement of what must be accomplished. A rally cry should run no longer than one sentence. It doesn't have to be perfect, but it does have to be motivational and directionally correct—like a campaign slogan.

Write out a sentence stating your goal. Then edit that sentence down to four or five words. You'll have a rally cry you can chant for the next ninety days.

One of my clients just challenged their project managers, project engineers, and superintendents to identify ten new potential sources of business. Their rally cry became: "Identify the top ten!" That's simple, straightforward, and easy to remember.

People tend to lose focus quickly. Giving your people a ninety-day rally cry will put what they need to accomplish in writing with credibility.

2. Initiatives

Initiatives are the concrete, objective tasks your direct reports will carry out to achieve their rally cry.

Clear initiatives give people focus, discipline, and confidence. Plus, they're specific actions you can hold them accountable for. Begin by nailing down which tasks you expect them to perform.

How do you determine these initiatives?

Once you've got a good rally cry, ask your people, "What steps do you need to accomplish to achieve your rally cry?"

Think of these steps as dominoes. Which domino will you knock down first? Which one falls second? Which one third? Line up a series of domino initiatives that will help drive the rally cry.

A client of mine wanted to improve field productivity. They tasked one of their direct reports with the rally cry "Implement training."

The first initiative was to build a skill matrix—a list of what each person needs to know to be considered well trained. The second initiative was to pick the training that would teach those skills. And the third initiative was to schedule the training.

Notice the domino effect: Build the skill matrix, choose the training based on it, then schedule the training.

List your top three initiatives to help achieve the rally cry.

3. Metrics

Once you've got a rally cry and a list of initiatives, the next step is to build your metrics. Metrics are objective indicators you are executing on the initiatives that will achieve the rally cry.

Let's talk about the types of metrics you might have on your ninety-day dashboard. They include leading indicators, lagging indicators, coincident indicators, and date-driven indicators.

A leading metric points toward future events. Let's say one of your direct reports has been tasked with the rally cry of improving safety. One of the initiatives is having consistent safety meetings.

Have those safety meetings taken place? The leading indicator is a simple yes or no. Because it's assumed that having safety meetings will reduce incidences and injuries on a project.

A lagging indicator confirms a pattern is in progress. Your experience modification rate (EMR) is one example. The EMR reflects your organization's injury claims and illness incidence over the past three years. So a lagging indicator shows what's happened in the past, but it can't tell you what's happening in the present.

That's why we use the next metric, a coincident indicator. Coincident indicators occur in real time and help you clarify what you're doing right now. One example of a coincident metric is your monthly accident and incident numbers.

Then we have the date-driven indicator metric. Date-driven indicators show if you're hitting deadlines. For example, I'm going to hold my first safety meeting by October 15.

Metrics are important because they make what's happening visible. That visibility allows you to have accountability conversations. The metrics will point toward issues you must resolve to achieve the rally cry. So make sure your direct reports are clear on the metrics linked to initiatives that drive the rally cry.

4. Relationships

This should go without saying, but it doesn't: The entire construction industry is driven by relationships. Without strong relationships, you will not have a strong construction business.

Relationships must be cultivated. They are key to achieving most initiatives in construction companies. When you're working with your direct reports, ask them whose help they need to achieve the rally cry.

They might need a mentor to point them toward achieving what's most important. Remember *The Empire Strikes Back*? Jedi-in-training Luke Skywalker traveled to a swamp planet to learn from Master Yoda. A Luke Skywalker in your company may need a more experienced adviser to achieve that rally cry.

Now let's say your rally cry has to do with business development. Perhaps your people need to cultivate relationships with a decision maker. They shouldn't just ask you to do it for them. You need to encourage your direct reports to think through who they need help from to achieve their rally cry.

5. Development Opportunities

Your company should be a place where folks are excited because they're advancing their careers. You want your people to always be developing and growing.

To encourage skill development, ask your direct reports, "What development opportunities do you need to help you achieve this rally cry?"

Maybe you think that if you develop your people and they leave, you've wasted time and money. Don't fall into that trap. Do your best to develop every single person in your organization. The best folks will stick around long term because you've shown you'll invest in their growth.

Next Steps

Every ninety days, go through the dashboard with your direct reports. That helps them focus, keeps them moving forward, and inclines them to contribute to your organization.

You might be thinking, *I don't have time for more tips and tricks!*

Reconsider that opinion in regard to this dashboard. It's not a trick; it's a tool. You have a responsibility to maximize your direct reports' impact in your organization. This tool is a simple way of helping them achieve high performance.

If you don't have consistent meetings with your direct reports, schedule recurring meetings. Explain the dashboard to them and ask them to fill it out.

It's important that they think the process through. Have them answer the questions. What is my rally cry? What are my initiatives? What do I need to do to achieve high performance?

In your first meeting with them after that, go through the dashboard step-by-step to make sure they understand each aspect. Then make your contribution.

The individual will probably aim in the right direction, but their rally cry or their initiatives may need some tweaks. You'll often find they're unclear on the metrics that are driving their success. Your job as a leader is to make crystal clear how they're being measured and evaluated.

After the meeting, agree on the final version of the dashboard. Give everyone a copy and use it as the foundation for all one-on-one conversations for the next ninety days. This will help your people make measurable progress. It will also enable you to hold them accountable. After ninety days, you can look back and see the progress you've made together. If your people achieve the rally cry, make sure you celebrate and recognize them.

Leading Your High-Performing Team

Once your measurements are in place and your team is improving, you need to know how to lead them. Next, let's look at the importance of one-on-one meetings with your direct reports and how to evaluate them all fairly.

One-on-One Meetings with Direct Reports

As you know by now, effective communication is essential to a high-performance team. The best construction companies are the ones that have a clear and consistent means of communicating information, surfacing and handling day-to-day problems, and identifying opportunities.

Communication improves by spending time together. Grab a piece of paper, write down the names of all the people who report directly to you, and then schedule a time to meet with each of them one-on-one within the next two weeks.

If you dread one-on-one conversations, then you may have poor relationships with your direct reports. That's exactly why you need to schedule these meetings.

In the leadership classic *High Output Management*, Andy Grove discusses the importance of a one-on-one meeting. His insights are the basis for the outline that follows.

Why do you need to have one-on-one meetings?

Invest Six Hours, and Get 480+ Hours of Impact

Deep, one-on-one meetings are an excellent way to leverage your time. If you spend one hour every two weeks with each of your six direct reports, your investment can impact 480+ hours of their work.

As you get out of the field more and more, you can lose some of your feel for the state of your business. One-on-one meetings let your direct reports "teach" you about current market conditions, the state of your crews in the field, and the nature of your company's relationship with suppliers, other building contractors, and owners.

You can use this time to both teach and learn. Drive home corporate culture by suggesting what you would do in a particular situation or what you've done in the past.

Don't Promote and Hope

Many construction companies struggle when they promote people from the field to the office or from labor to a supervisory role. Make sure you're meeting with people who are new to their roles as frequently as necessary so that you can say you've done everything in your power to help them to succeed in their new position.

How do you structure these meetings?

Time Frame, Location, Agenda

Set aside one hour for each one-on-one meeting. This is long enough to hear someone out and to let the real issues come to the surface.

Make it on their turf. It's their meeting, and you want them to feel as comfortable as possible. When meeting with a superintendent, if possible, go out to the site of your most critical current job; take a little time to walk it with them as a part of the meeting. This will give you a sense of how the job is running and give context to issues that come up. If you're in your direct report's office, you'll get an idea of how efficient and organized they are.

Construction is a tactile business and a people business. People design and build structures, and personal interaction is constant. Therefore, face-to-face meetings are best. Next best is a video chat so that you can still see their face and notice some nonverbal cues. If you can only meet by phone, discipline yourself to be in a place where there is no computer so that you can't be distracted by email or the internet.

Ask them to set the agenda. Have them email you an outline of three to five agenda items prior to the meeting so that you can print it out and bring it with you. Ask them to include critical numbers, how their people are doing, and the biggest challenges they're facing. Business is continually challenging. If they struggle to come up with items for the agenda, they're either hiding something or they're missing something in their area of responsibility.

Commit to taking written notes during your meeting. This will help you to focus on what your direct report is saying and will communicate to them that you take them seriously. Make sure you and your direct report commit to uninterrupted time.

Start with Numbers

You probably discuss critical numbers in the areas of bid, build, and bill in weekly meetings you have with your direct reports. The one-on-one meeting lets you take a deeper dive into the numbers. You can review an important estimate, or give feedback on more effective scheduling of a job, or even volunteer to make an accounts receivable call, if appropriate.

If you've already covered their agenda, or you need to keep the ball rolling, here are some questions to ask:

- What's the biggest challenge you're facing right now?
- Are you satisfied with your performance?
- Are you happy with your career path in the company?
- What are your main frustrations?
- What's the one thing I can do to help you do your job?

    Then ask them about their direct reports:

- Is anyone having struggles in their personal life that are affecting their job performance?
- Who needs additional training?
- Who's been improving?
- Who's been regressing? Knowing what you know now, would you still hire that person?

Also check in with each of your direct reports on the state of their relationships with your other direct reports. The one-on-one meeting is a great opportunity to surface issues.

At this point, there may be challenges that you know they haven't brought up yet. Make sure you do. Be specific, and ask them how they plan on handling the situation.

Peel the Onion

Like onions, people and problems have many layers to them. In a discussion, if you or your direct report begins to feel uncomfortable, that's often a sign you're getting closer to the truth. Keep asking questions. Never walk away from a meeting saying, "I should have asked them that question I was thinking about."

At the end of the meeting, make sure you and your direct report agree about any action items. Ask your direct report to include a write-up of those actions in your next one-on-one meeting.

Don't Make the Excuse of Being Too Busy

If you think that you don't have time for these conversations, reevaluate your schedule. Done right, these one-on-one meetings will save time and increase your leverage throughout your organization.

Start with one-on-one meetings with direct reports every other week. As you move forward, you can determine the ongoing frequency depending on the nature of your direct reports' job and how experienced they are. For example, if your senior estimator is working on a bid that is critical to your company's future, then you might want to meet with them on a weekly basis up until bid day so that you can provide them with any necessary input and support.

To recap, here's what you need to get started with one-on-one meetings:

1. List all your direct reports.
    a. Schedule a one-hour meeting with them within the next two weeks.
    b. Commit to holding that meeting regularly, every other week, for the next sixty days.
2. Have them prepare an agenda that includes the following:
    a. Critical numbers

       b.   People report

       c.   Biggest challenges

3.   Prepare your questions.

       a.   Print out the agenda.

       b.   Commit to uninterrupted time.

4.   Take notes.

       a.   Listen 80 percent of the time.

Conducting one-on-one meetings is just one part of your leadership duties. Next let's look at . . .

Evaluating Your Team

If you're the owner or the president of your company, this section is for you. If you're not, you'll still gain valuable insights from these pages, even if these decisions aren't up to you.

Most struggles in any organization stem from having the wrong people in the wrong seats or the right people in the wrong seats.

You want the right person in the right seat. Because your team is dynamic, your company is dynamic, and you should never settle.

You may have a wonderful year this year, but that does not guarantee a wonderful year next year. You may be satisfied executing one project at a high level, but you're only as good as your last project. And good performance requires a good team with everyone in the right place.

Sketch out where you sit in your organization and the people who report to you—they are your team. Your responsibility is to build a high-performing team.

Pick one role of someone who reports to you. Assign a score for how well that person performs that role. Ask yourself, "Do I have the right person in the right seat?"

Write down why the role exists. What is its core purpose? Don't think about the person who fills the role when you do this part. Think about the role itself.

Next, write down three to eight specific observable outcomes ranked by order of importance that the role should provide. After you do, look at your outcomes and ask yourself if they are observable. They should be objective, not subjective, outcomes.

Then write down three to eight descriptions of your culture that the person in this role must demonstrate. These are behaviors.

Culture mismatches often plague low-performing teams. Maybe someone can achieve outcomes but is not a cultural fit for your company. Such a person is in the wrong seat. But someone with the ability to execute on objectives who has the right behavior is in the right seat.

Again, ask yourself, "Do I have the right person in the right seat?"

Here's another measurement. If each team member walked into your office today and said, "I have an opportunity with someone else in the industry, and I'm going to take it," how would you respond?

Would you say, "Please don't go. Let's discuss any issues you might be facing," or would you express pleasure? Ask yourself that question for each team member. If you're glad someone is leaving, you don't have the right person in the right seat.

Maybe you think someone's right for the company but just needs to be put in the right seat. Or maybe you think more training and accountability are needed.

Those are acceptable answers. But here's the problem: In my work with construction executives and construction company CEOs, I ask them, "If we're still having the same conversation about this person in six months, do I have your permission to yell at you? Because I promise you, this is the biggest issue your company has."

It is not an easy problem to fix, sometimes due to a shortage of people or a shortage of specific talent. I'm not saying go out and fire all the wrong people in the wrong seats. I'm saying that your long-term commitment should be to improve your team and to never settle.

If you are a senior leader in your organization, you should be having your direct reports in your office for these conversations. You can still do this even if you're not a senior leader, because your direct reports have people reporting to them.

Always be evaluating your human talent. You might need to move them to different seats, you might need to train them, or you might need to give them an opportunity to find employment with other people.

You want to populate your organization with high performers. And you want to pay them well—so well they never want to leave. So well they work as hard as you. So well they want to buy the company from you one day. Yes, that's a possibility. Even a likelihood.

I'll show you how in the next chapter.

CHAPTER 5

INCENTIVIZING GREATNESS AND BUILDING FUTURE LEADERS

What if you had an incentive program that got the office and the field to work together as a more effective team? When you start an incentive program, you need to identify the outcomes you want. The role of each person in your company should be clearly structured yet free of micromanagement. Getting that balance just right can be tricky.

For a lot of folks in construction, structuring incentives is a big challenge. Why? Because they don't understand the difference between subjective and objective measurements of success.

Let's discuss how you can turn your incentive program into a morale booster—without confusing your employees or busting your bank account.

Compensate for Behaviors

Good teamwork starts with your hiring process. When you're filling roles, focus on the value people will bring to your organization. Rewarding that same value should flow into your incentive program. You'll create a golden thread that runs through an employee's career with your organization from start to finish.

If your incentive programs aren't working, odds are they reward behaviors you didn't hire people for. Employees whose job description lists outcomes one, two, and three shouldn't be incentivized to pursue outcomes four, five, and six. They'll neglect the job you hired them for just to get the extra money. Then you'll be paying incentives to employees you have to fire for not doing their jobs. Nobody wins in that situation. So how can you prevent a discrepancy between what you hire for and reward?

When you craft your job descriptions, always start with the value you want that role to add to your company. Then identify the duties and outcomes that provide that value. Build incentives that encourage your employees to accomplish tasks that provide this value. Now you have a clear job description at every interview, and your employees get a clear way of measuring their performance. No more miscommunication or uncertainty.

We all look out for ourselves. It's human nature. People do more of what gets them rewarded. When your incentive program encourages behaviors that benefit your company, both sides win. Give your employees the ability to look out for themselves and their families by improving their performance at the job you've hired them for.

Tensions may arise between what the company wants and what the employees want. When this happens, how do you align everyone's goals?

Come back to everyone's role within the company and what value you need from them. A field worker needs to provide optimal effort each hour in exchange for pay. But a project manager juggling tons of different job sites may be dealing with multiple factors that complicate the equation. Where can they both give their best effort? When is ROI optimized for the time they spend? Those are challenging questions because they have so many moving parts.

Employees in different areas of your organization may need different types of incentives. To structure incentives, look at each relevant employee and ask, "Where does this person have the most impact?" Then build the incentive around the answer. That may mean more tasks done per hour for field workers, more sales for the sales department, or more completion targets for project managers. Reward what you want each person doing.

As you structure incentives, make sure they're not blowing the budget. Remember your bottom line, but don't play Scrooge, either. A stingy approach leads to resentment and loss of morale. A too generous approach leads to everyone out of a job.

Tying Incentives to Achievable Goals

Achievable goals are the key to any incentive process. The worst idea is to base incentives on ideals your employee can never reach. If you set unattainable incentives, they'll get frustrated and say, "I can never get this bonus, so who cares?"

One of the biggest problems I see is owners setting incentives based on huge potential earnings. Everyone works as hard as they can, but the company doesn't hit that big number. Then everyone goes home empty-handed. How does that make employees feel? Not only did the company fail to achieve its goal but also the employees got nothing for all their effort. Worse, they may get lectured for failing to meet an unrealistic goal. If I were them, I'd find another job.

Part of your role is to get people excited about goals. We're motivators, and we have to keep our people hungry for their share of the pie.

Say you've got a three-year project. Do you wait until the end to pay incentives? Most people can't delay gratification that long. You may as well not pay an incentive at all.

Instead, consider paying an incentive each time the company gets paid. If the client is paying every ninety days, use that as your incentive marker.

Saying, "When I get paid, we all get paid" sends a loud message of shared prosperity to your team. It makes people more willing to take on long jobs. They now have multiple incentives paying out on the same project. How's that for motivation?

In short, don't incentivize people in the wrong direction, don't incentivize them for things they can't control, and don't hold back rewards so that they feel robbed. That's how you boost morale.

Preventing Bad Behaviors

There's an equal yet opposite problem, though. Let's say you're incentivizing sales. What keeps your sales team from selling to the wrong clients? This is a real concern because selling to a ton of bad clients can hurt the company. How do you balance incentives to control negative behavior?

Figuring out how to prevent bad behaviors means thinking like a lazy employee. If it were you, how would you play the system to get the most money while doing the least amount of work? You can even get the higher-ups in your company involved to help you try to game the system. Tweak your incentives until you can't see how to cheat anymore. And make sure you'd still feel eager to do a good job for the offered reward.

But how do you measure incentives?

In *High Output Management* by Andy Grove, the former Intel CEO discusses managing incentives in pairs. Instead of measuring only one behavior, measure two. That might mean tracking sales and repeat sales from return customers. The smaller incentive is for new customers, and the bigger incentive is for repeat business. This incentivizes the correct behavior, because your sales force will look for new customers who'll become repeat customers. A salesperson will earn two bonuses off one customer.

Leverage human nature to show your employees how doing the job right the first time pays off twice.

With your project managers, measure whether their projects come in on time, whether they come in with quality, how much rework they have to do, and how they adhered to safety requirements. Rewarding them only for finishing a project ahead of schedule might jeopardize safety and quality. Make sure you cover all desired behaviors.

What if a job requires one or more employees to shift certain tasks to outside of their control? Are they disqualified from earning incentives? Not if you structure them correctly. I'll explain how.

Incentivize to Encourage Sharing

If employees must shift duties to others outside of their control, reward that behavior by measuring overall outcomes. For example, that may mean basing (some, not all) incentives on how the whole company runs. This metric becomes more important as you move down from higher earners to lower earners. Tying some bonuses to your company's achievements incentivizes project managers, even if they don't have direct control over every element.

I'll put it another way. You're effectively shifting performance incentives from the individual to the whole (team, department, project manager) because employees and their managers may be unable to do their job without help, input, work, or oversight from others. Consider how some sales teams are paid commissions as a team rather than as a teammate, i.e., sales rep solely responsible for their own commission. What I'm really suggesting is incentivizing teamwork rather than "hogging the ball," so to speak.

Again, this approach incentivizes project managers in particular and everyone else in general to share knowledge. Because if you get paid more when the whole company does better, you'll want your coworkers to do a better job, too. It also rewards knowledgeable new members of your organization to streamline your processes. Do you want people keeping their mouths shut, or sharing solutions that can earn you more money in less time with better results?

Incentives don't have to be one or the other. You can incentivize based on individual job performance and company performance to get more of the behaviors you want. You'll just need to get creative so everyone is pulling for the goals of the company. How? With back testing.

Back Test Your Incentive Plan

One smart move when implementing a new plan is to figure out how it would work in the past. Sit down with the last five years of financial and project data, and determine how many bonuses would have been paid out already. Then look at how incentivizing those behaviors might have improved profits. Examine which incentivized behaviors may have prevented accidents, increased project speed, or helped you retain experienced workers who left for better pay.

Ensure that your incentives make sense. If you had a brutal down year, would you still pay out huge bonuses? No, because the morale boost wouldn't offset the damage to the company. But you do want to keep good workers when times are lean. There's a balance to be struck here, and back testing can help find it.

The best balance looks like everyone getting a small piece of a larger pie. Figure out how big your pie has been over the past five years and how much you could have afforded to dish out. Because dishing out the right amount could make the whole pie much larger. When that happens, everyone wins together.

While you're at it, weigh the pros and cons of setting up a company-wide incentive program instead of going one employee at a time. If you'd paid out your proposed incentives to every employee for the past five years, what would have changed? Would morale have gone up?

The answer may come down to communication.

Communicate Total Value

Incentive programs can be confusing to some employees. More so if you're targeting multiple behaviors with separate incentives while rewarding company-wide accomplishment. How do you communicate that mix?

Start by communicating the total value. What's the upper limit your workforce can achieve if they all pull together? Focus on the biggest benefit they can earn if they all work as a team in the optimal way. From there, zoom in on individual behaviors and how they fit together.

Your incentive programs shouldn't be random. They should flow from job descriptions. The global rewards should stem from company goals that each person is contributing to.

Communicate these incentives during hiring, because they're part of the benefits package. Communicating them to your team lets them know what to aim for and how to maximize their efforts for the best compensation.

This approach will also gain you new hires who want to work hard, because they know they're walking into a performance-based benefits package. The guys looking for an easy ride will avoid you. Just like you want.

But even the best incentive-driven workforce can be a double-edged sword if you make incentives subjective. Let's unpack what I mean.

Remove the Subjective Element

Let's say I'm a construction company president. I see we had a pretty good year, so I give Dave $30,000 and Fred $100,000. But next year, we have a downturn. Fred gets $5,000, and Dave gets a pat on the head. This is a terrible scenario that will obliterate employee morale.

Yes, it can feel good to pay subjective bonuses. Until people start to expect them. And it's far worse when events beyond your control force you to remove routine bonuses. Remember *National Lampoon's Christmas Vacation*? If you don't want to end up with an angry employee taking you hostage, or at least leaving the company, avoid subjective incentives.

How do you remove the subjective element from your incentive program and make it more objective?

Twelve smaller monthly payouts earn better emotional investment from your employees than one end-of-year lump sum. And you're more likely to retain good employees by rewarding good behavior at regular intervals instead of giving arbitrary bonuses at the end of the year. A lean month with low bonuses won't hit nearly as hard as a whole year with nothing.

Still set incentives on clear metrics tied to company performance. You share those metric measurements all year long, and you make sure everyone gets a share of the same pie at the end, not separate pies that pay out differently.

Reward payouts should never surprise anyone, because you've been clear on how to track them, what will be paid, and how things are proceeding at each stage. After all, how will you drive positive behaviors if you don't communicate how your people are doing? That's the whole point of performance-based initiatives.

Make sure your employees know that bonuses are tied to the company getting paid. You can't pay incentives from money you don't have. This means you need to maintain open communication each month about the status of incentives, where the money is, and what employees can expect. Be clear so that employees know how to earn the maximum bonus and when they can expect to get paid. That way they'll be more eager for the company to get paid. Let's look at an example.

Relations and Speed of Payment

If your accounts receivable folks know a payment is due, and their incentive is on the line, they'll contact the project manager (PM). A PM with an incentive also on the line will contact the client. The whole team works more effectively because they're rewarded for getting the job done. If you just paid out a year-end bonus, it would be your job to get the company paid.

Paying regular bonuses also incentivizes the whole team to be better at their jobs. If they cause problems that cost extra time to fix, everyone's incentives are held back. But by conducting themselves well on the job site, workers help everyone else get their incentives, too.

This approach makes employees more accountable and promotes pride in enriching everyone else with their labor. It also impacts the company's internal relations. People know who's pulling their weight and who's not. If your PMs and your foreman understand that they get paid when you get paid, they'll develop genuine care for the people around them. Because that attitude trickles up and affects their pay scales.

Trickling up is a process. To start raising your company's morale and production, let's look at where to start.

Trickling Up

Maybe now you're saying, "I want to implement an incentive program to boost employee morale and company productivity, but I've never done one before. If it's too late to start at the hiring process, where *do* I start?"

Begin by looking at the people you want to retain. Chances are they're the people at the top of your company who keep the whole operation running. If you want to keep them, build incentive programs for them as I outlined earlier. Then work your way down the list to your other employees.

This method allows you some leeway and experimentation as you go. Roll out your incentives with a smaller headcount first to see what happens. Target the people who need them the most. That way you can manage the inevitable mistakes. You're leveraging human nature, and to err is human.

Have frank conversations with your upper-level staff. Tell them you're trying incentive pilot programs. Ask for honest feedback, and tell them you'll make adjustments as you go to ensure that both sides benefit. If you give them more agency, they'll be more willing to help you adjust.

This also prevents communication failures from the top down. Your upper management won't fracture into separate projects if collective effort determines their incentives. By tying your highest-level employees together, you can unify your company much faster. And it will keep you grounded, which is more important than you may think. Let me explain why.

Humility

You won't get this perfect on your first try. Remain humble, and maintain open communication with your team about ongoing adjustments to incentives.

Don't be the big CEO who screws over the smallest guys in the company and brushes it off. Tell your employees if you make it harder to earn rewards so as not to hurt the company. People want big rewards, but they also want to stay employed. Besides, the ability to say, "This was my mistake" is a part of leadership. People respect a leader who takes ownership of problems.

When you roll out your pilot program, set a time cap on how long the incentives will run. Try three or six months. Explain that if all goes well, you'll consider extending it. Get feedback throughout the process, and be honest in communicating with the team. Your incentive program should have full transparency and zero shocks.

There are three main benefits to a well-structured incentive program. One, it helps you retain your key people. Two, it improves communication and reduces friction between departments. And three, it improves performance. But it only works if you stay humble and take feedback.

So stay open to your team. A good boss who cares about mutual benefit is one of the best incentives. Make sure your company has that kind of leadership. I'll show you how next.

From One Generation to the Next: How to Prepare Tomorrow's Leaders Today

Incentives help build morale. They can also encourage people to take on leadership roles as they motivate one another to strive for shared incentives. This is an added benefit of proper incentive programs. They separate those who are hungry and driven to perform from those just showing up for a paycheck. Once you've implemented your incentive program, it should be easier to distinguish who's qualified for leadership.

But what if you want to take a more direct role in shaping leadership inside your company? Maybe it's time to step back and take a less active role as you promote someone else to management. If that's the case, you need to get your selection just right. And you need to approach it in the smartest way.

Here are my top suggestions for handling new leaders you bring up through your organization.

Prepare for Your Conversation

When you're considering leadership candidates inside your organization, be honest about their performance. That requires a frank assessment of them as employees.

Yes, someone might be a good PM. But are better PMs available? Are the candidate's metrics all excellent? It's not enough to do a decent job. You don't want decent leaders; you want great leaders.

Remember, leadership is about more than numbers. How are the candidate's relationships with clients and subordinates? Is there good communication with others? Don't promote someone into leadership who can't work with a team.

Make sure all candidates understand their current role. Do they understand the job well enough to explain it in simple terms? Are they clear about their performance measurements and know why they're important? Do they see how they fit into the big picture?

Last but not least, how eager is the candidate to do a good job? Does this person show up and put in the minimum time and effort, or do they give 100 percent every minute on the job? Does the candidate cap out every incentive program and drive the company to higher profits?

If you want to hand off leadership of your company, look for people who can execute, who are entrepreneurial, and who have experience in hiring and team building. You also want people who aspire to leadership. Follow these suggestions to find the best fit for the whole company.

Embrace Circumstance

When selecting leadership to work under or eventually replace you, you need to know they're made of stern stuff. That means seeing how they adapt to different circumstances.

Do they rise to challenges? Think back to the last time you saw something not go their way. How did they react? Did they blame everyone else and throw a tantrum, or did they take ownership and make a plan? Are they easily discouraged? Or do they embrace their circumstances and find the best possible outcome?

Speaking of circumstances, how do they feel about their job? And about leadership? Do they have a passion for the work? Are they just following any opportunity, or are they in construction because they love it? Passion can carry the day even when times are hard. A good leader needs to want the job done when others want to quit.

What about fear? How does your candidate deal with it? Fear can be good if it drives a person to work harder and pay attention to quality. Pressure gives us diamonds, after all. Does this person thrive or crumble under it?

Relationships and Communication

Pay attention to how your candidate relates to others and communicates with them. This determines everything about a leader.

How do they speak to those above, on par, and below them? Are they respectful? Friendly? Snippy or rude? Do they waste time on gossip? The way they communicate says a lot about the culture they'll create if you give them a place at the top.

Communication style determines a lot about the relationships your potential leader will establish within and outside the company. If you put this leader in front of your clients and employees, will you look better or worse than you do right now? Can the candidate be trained to communicate differently? A rude communicator may have a personality issue, but an uncertain communicator can learn the skills to be a great communicator.

Be honest about what people bring to the table.

Design the Company You Want

The goal of incentives and leadership promotions is to shape your workforce into the company you envision.

We talked about vision and goals in the last couple of chapters. Align them with the behaviors you're rewarding and the type of leaders you're putting in place. If you aim to get things done right when other companies fail, don't promote the guy who puts speed over safety and quality. Instead, promote leaders who value a culture of attentiveness and reward employees who prioritize quality work and client satisfaction.

It's all about shaping your company to be what you want it to be. That comes down to rewarding your people. Make sure you're incentivizing and promoting in alignment with your vision.

Don't forget the importance of communication in achieving your goals and promoting your vision. We'll discuss that next.

CHAPTER 6

GIVE THEM AN EAR: HOW GREAT LEADERS COMMUNICATE

I f you want to remember everything you need to communicate to your people every day, you only have to grab your EAR.

E stands for encouragement, *A* for accountability, and *R* for recognition. In other words, "You can do it. Did you do it? You did it!"

I know, I know, that's cheesy. Even so, if you want to remember the three most important messages you must communicate to your team every day, use this cute mnemonic device. All you have to do is *grab your ear*.

In order to get the most from the EAR framework, there are three things I encourage you to do.

One, drop the mask. I mean with yourself. If you get good at telling yourself the truth, your life will go much better.

Two, ditch the attitude. I'm not a rocket scientist. I don't have a PhD. It's not what we know; it's what we do that builds our character. So even if you know it all, ask how well you're applying that knowledge.

Three, kill the bear. In the movie *The Edge*, Anthony Hopkins is rich with a hot wife. Alec Baldwin wants the money and the woman. Thanks to movie magic, they end up in the wilderness pitted against a bear. The plot is simple. Either they kill the bear or the bear kills them. Anthony Hopkins has never killed a bear before, but he knows that someone somewhere has. And he says this: "What one man can do, another man can do."

If what you read in this chapter and those ahead leaves you thinking, *Oh man, I should have done that fifteen years ago!* Or *I could never do that*, remember: If someone's done it before, so can you.

Now you're ready to learn the EAR framework.

The EAR Framework, Explained

Let's review what EAR means:

- Encouragement
- Accountability
- Recognition

Ancient Greek and Roman armies had a position called the Paraclete, or comforter. The Paraclete would put his arm around his fellow soldiers as they were going into battle and encourage them by saying, "You can do it." And as they were in the battle, he would hold them accountable by asking, "Did you do it?" Then, after the battle, he would recognize them by saying, "You did it."

You can do it. Did you do it? You did it. Those are the three messages you need to be consistent in communicating to those you lead.

Think about your organizational chart and your direct reports. Who needs encouragement? Who needs accountability? Who needs recognition? Identify those people, and have the corresponding conversations with them.

If you haven't held someone accountable based on performance in the last month, that's a lapse in leadership. Likewise if you haven't recognized someone for a job well done.

That's the EAR framework. Let's explore each part.

Encourage

Aside from a simple, "You can do it," how do you encourage your people? What professional and personal struggles do they face?

First of all, make sure you're rewarding the behavior you want to see repeated. That means encouraging the right people in the right roles. Pushing ambitions on people who don't share your hopes just makes them angry. Back your encouragement with the right mindset. That's how you direct your people in the right actions.

Always be transparent in the motives behind your encouragement. People are desperate to know the why. That deep sense of understanding is essential for excellence.

Think about encouraging people in terms of their performance. Like we discussed earlier, high performance is concentrating on tasks that, if done with excellence, have a significant impact on individual and group outcomes. You can encourage the outcomes that each of your direct reports must achieve in order to succeed.

One of my clients is a young guy at an office that just opened in Reno. He's dealing with tons of distractions. So I asked him recently, "What are your top three outcomes?"

He answered right away. "Develop relationships, bid and win work, build it successfully."

You want to ask your people the same question and get clear answers like those. For example, your superintendents and foremen need to be safe, fast, and do high-quality work.

Once you've got your people's answers, pinpoint the one outcome that adds the most value to your company. Then identify the primary three tasks responsible for that top outcome and pick the most important one. Now ask your direct reports, "In what specific ways can you improve your performance of this task?"

Letting your people think through how they can improve their performance is vital to encouraging them. As a leader, you should walk your subordinates through the tasks that generate the outcomes you expect. Tell them, "You can do it."

Maybe you have one direct report who has potential but whose job performance is a little shaky. You need to sit down together and make sure it's crystal clear what must be done to achieve high performance. Again, identify expected outcomes and the tasks that lead to them. Pick the most important task, and invite your direct report to think, "How can I improve my performance of this task in the next thirty days?"

Then look that person in the eye and say, "You can do it." Of course, encouragement alone isn't enough. Let's talk about accountability.

Accountability

What is accountability? It's holding people responsible for their actions and outcomes within their realm of responsibility and corresponding with their authority. It sounds easy, but accountability can be derailed by stealth obstacles. Let's look at a few.

Time

Chances are, your biggest obstacle to holding people accountable will be time. Having a tight deadline makes it hard to delegate, because you feel like no one else will get tasks done on schedule.

Heroism

In chapter 2 of this book, we called out three behaviors that cause construction leaders to get in their own way. Two of these are recurring issues I've had to help clients surmount over and over, so I bring them up again here. They're heroism and perfectionism.

As a leader, of course you want to be the hero. Your people love it when you come flying in and save the day. And you love the buzz that comes from their admiration. But that buzz will hinder your ability to pass your company on to others.

Perfectionism

Recall from chapter 2 that perfectionists find it difficult to hold others accountable. For example, you may think nobody can do it as well as you, and you may be right. But that's not the point. Who decides what's good enough? The customer does. Not you.

I'm not saying you should lower your expectations or standards. Maybe you can do it better than 90 percent of the people in your organization. But that doesn't matter. What matters is if your people can do it well enough to satisfy the customer.

Mistrust

You might say, "The last time I delegated to someone, they screwed it up and I had to take over anyway. Now I know better than to trust people."

If you struggle to trust people, you'll resist giving them tasks to begin with. That's why delegation is the flipside of mistrust and a key part of accountability.

A Quick Delegation Framework

Choose which tasks you're willing to delegate. Pick the best person to delegate them to. Give them clear, detailed instructions. Then set a completion date. This lets you delegate responsibility and authority, not just the task.

How do you decide which tasks to delegate? Think of one thing you're doing right now but shouldn't be. Someone else should be doing it, but you're a perfectionist who avoids the hard work of teaching it to others. Stop doing it.

One November day, I said to my wife, "Come January, I'm not doing the dishes anymore."

Here's why. I know my wife and I can do the dishes better than our kids. We've been doing them for years. But the kids can do the dishes themselves. I drew a line in the sand while giving us a little time to teach the kids. How did it go? It's been awesome. Now they're doing the dishes, and it's good enough.

When you're delegating, ask yourself, "Am I clear about what I'm delegating? Does this person understand what needs to be done? Is this person capable of achieving the outcome I want?" These questions help you fill in any missing information for a more favorable outcome.

Beware of Abdication

While some leaders have trouble delegating, others have the opposite problem. They love delegating—to the ones in their company who stay late and get everything done. But at a certain point those workhorses reach overcapacity, and their performance goes down. So take your people's capacity into account, and spread the delegation around. Because otherwise you're abdicating, not delegating.

Maybe you understand how to delegate, but holding your people accountable is still a challenge. A simple and effective solution is to have accountability conversations.

An accountability conversation should include three questions: "Did you do it? If not, what got in the way? How can I help?" That's all it takes to hold people accountable.

Who in your company needs accountability? Make a list of anyone and everyone who could benefit from this conversation. Once you have your list, don't wait until next month to hold those people accountable. Have those conversations today.

Just as important is recognizing the people who've reached (or surpassed) your outcome expectations. Let's explore how.

Recognition

Think back to a time when you were recognized for a job well done. How did it feel? Pretty great, right? Others feel the same when you recognize them for the work they do.

To be effective at recognition, you have to be specific, personal, and consistent. We live in a cheap recognition culture where people sometimes get recognized just for showing up. I'm not talking about that.

Back when I was just starting my career, I worked as the lead generator for an entrepreneurial company selling copiers. One of the owners used to pull me aside at the end of the week and say something like "Eric, I really like what you did over here on Wednesday. It was awesome!" It meant the world to me every time.

Why? Because it was personal. When I won Marketer of the Year, it was impersonal, because I was the only person in the marketing department. But when my employer gave me a plaque with the specific amount I'd sold, I ran home and said to my wife, "Let's put this on the wall!"

Who in your organization needs specific, personal recognition? Maybe there are people you haven't spoken to in a while. Stop by and recognize them for the work that they do. It can have a tremendous impact. Everyone wants to feel appreciated.

Before you give recognition, be aware that not everyone likes to be recognized in the same way. Some people are humiliated if they're brought in front of a crowd. Other people love the spotlight. Some people just want a face-to-face conversation. You don't even have to give them a bonus. Just look them in the eye and tell them you appreciate them. Those moments stick with people for years.

So as you're grabbing your EAR and thinking about encouragement and accountability, remember to give recognition where it's needed.

To be meaningful, consistent, and fair, recognition needs to be based on standards. What standards should every construction company strive for? Read on.

Seven Attributes of the Best Construction Leaders

I have a friend who's been in the construction industry for thirty years. He got laid off recently because his employer had a major financial loss on one of their projects.

Now my friend is a kick-ass project manager and estimator. So how'd he get laid off in the middle of a booming economy?

You might remember I mentioned the seven attributes of effective strategy in construction companies, which I learned from *The Construction MBA* by Matt Stevens. My friend got laid off because his employer lacked these seven attributes. I've adapted them slightly as a guide for construction leaders.

1. They pursue niche work at which they are excellent and profitable.
2. They deal with clients they know well.
3. They work with project partners they trust.
4. They maintain high-quality, efficient construction work.
5. They emphasize and demand safety.
6. They insist on timely payment for all dollars earned.
7. They have a financial cushion.

Let's reconsider these seven attributes where *you* are concerned. Reflect on ones that you do well and on ones you need to improve. Think about the up-and-coming people in your organization. Who is one of your direct reports that you've pinned some hopes on?

Does that person understand these seven attributes? If not, can you teach them so that they can be an effective construction leader? According to David Foster Wallace, a real leader can help others overcome their laziness, selfishness, weakness, and fear.

Don't think you're immune to those things. We all face challenges. The best leaders meet and overcome those challenges. Using the EAR framework not only helps you overcome laziness, selfishness, weakness, and fear but also helps you lead others to conquer them.

Time for a brief example from history. In 1805, Napoleon was poised to conquer England. His French and Spanish galleons met the English fleet at Trafalgar. To fight naval battles back then, each side would line up and close in on the other while firing on the enemy's ships. And when they got close enough, they'd board one another's ships and hack each other to death.

If the English had done that, they would have been wiped out by Napoleon's better-armed galleons. So Nelson, the English admiral, came up with a different approach.

The English were better shots, and the soldiers on their boats were efficient fighters. So Admiral Nelson and his commanders planned to cut the enemy lines in half with their smaller, lighter boats, board the Spanish galleons, and take them out.

Let's examine what Nelson did right as a leader. Number one, he had a clear command intent. His captains understood how they were to execute the battle. Number two, he picked competent decision makers to whom he could delegate crucial tasks. Number three, he had his men gather rich information about the battle space and share it. And number four, he fostered mutual trust at all levels of command.

Working with contractors since 2004 has convinced me that what separates winners from losers is the leadership team's communication. For better or for worse, your company reflects you and your ability to communicate with those you lead.

Think about your immediate successor. Is there room for improvement in some area? Which one? How well does this person communicate? Now think about the people who report to you. How many of them do you trust? How many of them trust you?

Life is a battle. That's why you must fill your company's chain of command with competent, trustworthy decision makers to secure its future.

Bringing competent people on board is only half the battle. The other half is keeping them. The EAR framework can help you retain top talent. Here's how.

The EAR Legacy

Remember my hypercompetent friend who was laid off? He got three offers from other companies. One offer came from a corporation, another from a company out of the Bay Area, and another from a local business. The local firm offered him two or three dollars an hour less than the corporation, but he picked the local organization because of the culture fit.

It's your culture that will keep the best people. And the best organizations are those that recognize high performers appropriately. That's where the EAR framework comes in.

Recall the Battle of Trafalgar. The Spanish and the French together intended to invade Britain under Napoleon's command. But there was Admiral Nelson, who, instead of attacking head-on, led the English navy toward their foes from a diagonal angle of attack. Britain destroyed twenty-one Spanish and French ships while losing none of their own. But the English suffered one substantial loss—Admiral Nelson. He died to win that battle.

Consider how much you've sacrificed to build your construction company. Are you going to hand down that legacy? Nelson's column stands in Trafalgar Square in London as the legacy of his leadership. What we do today impacts future generations, for better or for worse.

Think about the quality of your leadership and the messages you're communicating to your direct reports. To cement your legacy, give your people your EAR.

This same leadership quality and messaging can be applied to time spent in meetings. I'll show you how in the next chapter.

CHAPTER 7

RUN KICK-ASS MEETINGS

I t's frustrating when you call a meeting but your team struggles to reach an agreement on how to solve a problem. You might think it's because they don't want to come to consensus or because you're failing as a leader. Most of the time, neither reason is the case. The issue is most likely your meeting structure, not that anyone in your company sucks at running meetings and giving action items during those meetings or even wanting to hold actionable meetings in the first place. It's structure. Change your meetings' structure, change your company's future.

In this chapter, you'll learn a simple meeting structure that will lead your team to a unanimous agreement on how to solve a problem in less than thirty-seven minutes.

Consider the alternative—running time-wasting meetings that result in no agreement, no actions taken afterward, and no desirable outcomes achieved. That's what your competitors are up to, probably with no vision to change it, either. It's not like the necessity for a new way to do meetings doesn't exist, though. Everyone hates going to lousy meetings. In case you need some convincing, check out these statistics from TED.com[1]:

---

1 - Emily Pidgeon, "The Economic Impact of Bad Meetings," TED, November 17, 2014, https://ideas.ted.com/the-economic-impact-of-bad-meetings.

- Twenty-five percent of meetings are spent discussing irrelevant issues.
- Fifty percent of people find meetings to be unproductive.
- Seventy-three percent of employees do other work in meetings.
- Ninety percent of people daydream in meetings.
- One hundred percent of employees play Candy Crush, Snapchat with friends, or text their kids during meetings.

OK, that last one was a joke. But you get the idea. Executives average twenty-three hours a week in meetings, which means that 7.8 hours of that time is spent in unnecessary or mismanaged meetings. That's over two wasted months a year, per executive.

Do the math. If you're paying a group of five executives an annual average of $100,000, that adds up to $83,333 of wasted salary per year. Project those numbers over ten years, and you can see how bad meetings can cost you millions of dollars in payroll alone.

How many hours have you wasted in meetings that failed to address the real issues that affect your company? Do you talk and talk but never take action? Or if you do take action, are you focusing on real solutions?

If you're shamefully nodding, it's not your fault. Seventy-five percent of leaders receive zero formal training on how to conduct a well-structured meeting. They don't know how to begin with a bang, how to tap into the attendees' best thinking, or how to drive toward a conclusion in a timely manner.

Every business needs meetings to discuss overcoming challenges. The problem is that most meetings are too time-consuming, too rigid, or too chaotic. Most leaders lack the skills to gather ideas so that bias and preconceived notions don't squelch creativity. Nor can they narrow those ideas down to one the team can commit to implementing. How do you tackle these problems?

As you might expect by this point in the book, there's a simple solution.

The concept of kick-ass meetings (KAM) is a straightforward, three-step process that helps you address these specific issues and empowers you to run killer meetings that people *look forward* to attending. KAM lets you present a problem to your team and lead them through brainstorming, prioritization, and action planning.

KAM provides the structure to keep your meetings on track and on time without the stifling rigidity of agenda-driven formats. In less than an hour and on one page, you'll generate a clear, three-part action plan that can hold people accountable. You'll be able to instill a problem-solving, action-oriented bias that helps drive your business to success and profit.

KAM consists of three parts: idea generation, prioritization, and action planning. But before you can use KAM at your next meeting, you have to do a little preparation.

Preparing

Identify the Problems within the Four Ps

What is the source of the business problems you usually face?

Like every business, you offer a product. You have a unique business process that guides every aspect of your operation. You have employees (people) who help drive your success. All these work together to maximize profit. These are the four Ps: product, process, people, and profit.

If you have problems with any aspect of your product, process, or people, your profit will suffer. The market doesn't lie, and it will punish you for poor service or failure to deliver. So where are the majority of your problems?

Numbers and Conversations

One of the best ways to discover where problems are is to track your operations. The best businesses measure every aspect of their daily operations. They track customer loyalty, employee retention, product quality, sales and marketing activities, and financial data.

Of course, not everything is measurable. That's why it's vital to communicate with your executive team and every department about the health of their internal relationships (i.e., coworkers). By narrowing your focus to product, process, and people, then tracking numbers and maintaining open and frequent communication, you'll identify what problems you need to address. Once you've identified a problem, you must choose who to involve in the problem-solving process.

Gather the Team

Gathering the right problem-solving team can be tricky. You have to strike a balance between quality and quantity. First, invite the leaders the problem affects, then add anyone who can give technical input from a process-based perspective. Depending on the topic, you may also invite someone without a deep technical background or from a different department, just to get an outsider view.

For example, you may bring someone from marketing or sales to a meeting about project management. You'll get a unique perspective from those who engage with your customers regularly.

Whatever mix you choose, don't have too many participants. I recommend between six and ten—but not more than twelve. This gives you diversity of input without too many viewpoints muddying the waters.

Once you've decided who's coming to the meeting, it's time to hold a kick-ass one.

The Kick-Ass Meeting Formula

Make the Rules

Your job as the meeting leader is to keep the process running smoothly, with ground rules for participation. Here are the three rules that will ensure an effective meeting:

1. No distractions. Put away your phones for the entire length of the meeting.
2. No dismissing ideas. Suspend judgment regarding the validity of ideas. No laughing at, mocking, or belittling others' input.

3. Everyone participates. No one gets to hide in the corner, and no one gets to dominate. Everyone who's there was invited because they have something to contribute. If someone is lying low, ask them questions. If someone is dominating, ask questions of others.

Meetings are about ideas. Let's look at how to cultivate the right ones for your situation.

Idea Generation

Brainstorming is an overused word, but it's a vital aspect of KAM. You don't know the future, so you can't be 100 percent certain about what will work. But you can use a combination of data, experience, and intuition to generate as many ideas as possible. This helps you choose a course of action to address the problem. Here are three steps that will help you conduct a successful brainstorming session.

Step 1: Frame the Problem Clearly

Frame the problem as a question, such as:

- "In what specific ways can we improve our marketing?"
- "In what specific ways can we eliminate waste during production?"
- "In what specific ways can we function more effectively as a leadership team?"
- "In what specific ways can we increase customer retention?"

Using the word *specific* helps people answer more precisely, producing more actionable ideas.

Step 2: Set a Two-Minute Timer

Make sure that everyone understands the question and agrees that it's relevant. Then set a timer for two minutes. Have all participants write down as many answers to the question as they can think of in that time.

Encourage them by affirming that there are no bad ideas and that the key is quantity, not quality. This takes the pressure off. Remind them that you're looking for specific answers that can be acted upon.

Step 3: Narrow the Ideas

Right after the two-minute brainstorming session, have each participant look at their list and pick the top two ideas. They can choose only two each. If someone has only two, no problem. Even one is acceptable if that's all someone can think of.

Once you have completed the idea generation phase, you're ready to gather those ideas. This is the toughest yet most interesting part of KAM.

Step 4: Gather the Ideas

Go around the room and ask for the first idea from each participant. Tell them to be as specific as possible. Make a numbered list of these ideas on a flip chart or whiteboard where everyone can see it and then discuss them.

Don't allow one person to dominate. It's OK to interrupt monologues and discuss the point with the group. Asking questions gives you control of the conversation and helps others make their points succinctly.

After you have one idea from each attendee, start over and get the last person's second idea. It's fine if some duplicates turn up. Thank those who make redundant contributions, and ask if they'd like to enhance or expand upon their ideas in specific ways.

Four Facilitation Secrets

1. One at a Time

Most people will have (at least) two ideas they want to share. Insist upon courtesy and self- control, and take only one idea at a time. Let the eager beavers know you'll get their additional ideas after others have shared. This way you give everyone a chance to contribute.

2. Get Out of the Way

The meeting facilitator's goal is to bring out the best in others, not dominate the conversation. Don't judge the ideas on the board. At this point there are no bad ideas.

3. Shut Up

Some people need time to talk through their thoughts. So let them talk. Practice active listening skills. When concentrating on listening, I like to ball up the toes on my right foot. It creates a mild physical tension that helps me focus on what the other person is saying. I combine the physical action with an internal verbal cue: *Ground yourself.* This reminds me to shut down the conversation in my head and pay complete attention to what is being said.

4. Reframe

Ask questions to reframe the ideas if necessary, but do not shut someone down and move on until you're sure you've heard the whole idea.

After everyone has had two opportunities to provide input, ask, "Are there any other ideas anyone would like to add?"

A few more suggestions may pop up. Depending on the group's size, you'll end up with a list of six to twenty-four ideas. Some of them will be good, some will be average, and some will be less helpful.

This is where most people stop. They look at the board, feel good about having gotten something done, and adjourn the meeting. Big mistake. Remember the saying about meetings: "When all was said and done, a lot was said and nothing was done." It's time to prioritize those ideas.

Prioritization

Even if every idea is awesome, you'll never get to implement them all. The more you talk and the less you act, the more your credibility as leader and the morale of your team will suffer.

It's time to slash the list. Ask each participant to choose the best third of the ideas displayed. If you have fifteen ideas, instruct everyone to pick the best five. This way everyone gets to see the list, and because people will have already contributed, they'll be willing to consider others' input. They can choose the best ideas, even if they are not their own.

After everyone has chosen their top ideas, gather the votes. The big mistake some facilitators make here is to go around the room asking everyone to share the ideas they picked. This allows people to see which ideas are popular.

Instead, point to idea number one and ask, "By a show of hands, who selected this idea?" That will speed up vote gathering and keep people from second-guessing themselves. If the majority (or a tie) have that idea in their top five (or top third), it stays. If they don't, draw a line through it to cross it off the board. Go down the whole list of ideas this way.

Next, have the participants select their top idea from the remaining list. About 80 percent of the time, one idea will come out with a majority of the votes. And about 20 percent of the time, two or three ideas will receive an equal number of votes. When that happens, ask the participants to pick their top idea. If everyone *had* to select one and only one, which is it?

Keep in mind that you want to build an action plan, and choosing one idea is vital to clear planning. Don't try to select the perfect idea. Seek team agreement and commitment.

Getting Commitment

Once the winning idea has surfaced, address the meeting participants. "This idea has received the most votes. By a show of hands, how many of us are willing to leave this meeting committed to implementing it in the next thirty days?" Adjust the time frame within reason to fit the problem you're addressing.

I have used this process since 2004 to run brainstorming sessions at many levels of organizational complexity. And I have never failed to get unanimous commitment. How? It's simple—everyone has had the chance to contribute ideas and then choose the best one. If you have good employees committed to your business, they will be happy to rally around the best ideas for solving your toughest challenges.

I guarantee you that the energy in a roomful of those people will be high. Don't be fooled by that energy. It will fade fast and must be funneled into organized action. Read on to learn how.

Action Planning

We're on the last step of KAM. Idea generation got the team thinking about how to solve the problem and allowed everyone to give input. Prioritization gave everyone a chance to choose the best idea. Now that you've chosen your top idea, it's time for you and your team to make a plan to overcome the problem.

Get Your Boots Muddy

Great companies have a bias for intelligent, specific action. Action is everything.

I love General George Patton's statement, "A good plan violently executed now is better than a perfect plan next week." Patton was a "muddy boots" general in World War II. He spent plenty of time planning and discussing his attacks, but when it was time to move, he was on a tank with the troops charging forward.

Most business leaders are nothing like Patton. Too many companies lack a plan to guide them while they work to overcome their problems. Or they make their plans too complicated and hard to implement. KAM includes a simple three-part action planning process that will get you moving forward: the rally cry, fierce focus, and critical numbers.

Rally Cry

Remember the rally cry from chapter 4? If you've done a good job identifying and articulating the best idea, this part will be simple—so simple that you can probably guess what I'm about to say next. Please read on anyway, though, to prove yourself right.

You'll take your best idea and translate it into a word or short phrase, like a campaign slogan that illustrates your goal. Build this rally cry around what needs to happen for the problem to be addressed.

One of my construction company clients just used KAM to generate ideas on how to improve their operations. After the generating ideas process, they selected: "Emphasis on cost control, tracking, and forecasting." They translated this idea into the clear rally cry "Own the cost."

Fierce Focus

Sales, marketing, production, and finance are the major areas you'll focus on to achieve your rally cry. Fierce focus will help you identify what needs to be done and who will be responsible for doing it.

So what specific actions will implement your team's idea and solve your problem?

Who needs to perform these actions?

After identifying "Own the cost" as their rally cry, my client chose three areas of fierce focus:

1. Project managers set up the job for margin success.
2. Superintendents develop the lowest possible cost and optimize resources.
3. Foremen execute at the lowest possible cost.

Keep it simple. Simple actions help you set metrics, which we'll get into next.

Critical Numbers

The last stage of the action planning process is numbers—the metrics you must track to determine whether your areas of fierce focus are being executed.

To achieve the "Own the cost" rally cry, my client chose to focus on the following:

- Project manager: margin growth
- Superintendent: equipment utilization
- Foreman: cost per unit installed

Each project manager, superintendent, and foreman was held accountable by tracking the critical numbers associated with each area of fierce focus. Don't worry if this example doesn't apply to your business directly. Just identify the numbers you need to track, and tie them to your areas of fierce focus.

Wait, Why Is This So Hard?

The action planning process I just described is effective but only if you use it consistently. The reason many business leaders are ineffective at solving problems is that they don't hold others accountable.

Accountability is painful for everyone involved. It can incite conflict that most would rather avoid. But the only way to tackle a problem is to identify it, figure out the best way to solve it, build a plan, and hold people accountable for the execution of that plan.

You can do this effectively by holding regular meetings during which you review the critical numbers and hold people accountable to the rally cry as they execute their areas of fierce focus. When you hold these meetings and identify a problem that's hindering the rally cry, use KAM again to determine how you'll remove that obstacle. When holding others accountable, avoid questions like "Why didn't you do this?" Instead, try "What got in the way of accomplishing this, and what do you need to get it done?"

What happens when you implement this process? In the case of my construction client, they had their most successful year in over a decade.

Time to Move

You'll get value from KAM as soon as you put them into action. Look at your numbers and identify a recurring problem you've had trouble addressing. Assemble a group to address the problem. Ask specific questions to generate, gather, and prioritize ideas. Then build an action plan with the rally cry, fierce focus, and critical numbers. Problem solved.

KAM will empower you to run efficient meetings with the structure to keep participants on track and the flexibility to keep them engaged.

Commit to holding your people accountable for implementation. Be flexible and willing to pivot if you need to. And keep using KAM to advance through the problem-solving process to build a more profitable business. KAM will help you run an effective meeting and bring your team to an agreement on how to solve your toughest challenges.

PART 2:
CONSTRUCTION STRATEGY

CHAPTER 8

THE FOUR Ps THAT BUILD THE COMPANY OF YOUR DREAMS

Walmart has a clear purpose that drives what they do: to uplift the quality of life for working-class people by offering the same products rich people buy at affordable prices.

Providing this kind of clarity and motivation is leadership. If you can't do it yet, this is where you'll learn.

Having a purpose helps set you apart from the competition. It improves the quality of your daily decisions. And it can appeal to your employees' deepest motives, unleashing their enthusiasm. In short, having a mission helps you find the energy you need for the daily grind.

Your personality also sets you apart. So do your values. But have you thought those values through and communicated them in a way that builds a culture around them?

This chapter will explore your purpose, your values, and your leadership—and how those things affect your company culture. Let me show you how to identify the unique offer your company provides and how to communicate that to your team in a way that boosts their daily momentum. Much of what follows is inspired by Patrick Lencioni's book *The*

Advantage: Why Organizational Health Trumps Everything Else in Business. So if you like what you read and want more on these topics, I recommend Patrick's book as your next read after you finish *Construction Genius*.

Purpose

Every car on the road exists for the same basic purpose—to transport people. But a deeper purpose underlies many car owners' choice of vehicle. Which words spring to mind when you think of your car? Safe? Reliable? Affordable? Powerful? Fun? The deeper purpose for a car depends on how it's built and the driver's motives, perceptions, and feelings about driving it.

When I first met my wife, she drove an SUV. It was perfect for the ski trips we used to take. After we got married and had kids, we switched to a Honda Odyssey minivan. It ended up with coffee, food, and all kinds of other stains inside. Then a couple of years ago, I traded up to a GMC Yukon. My wife was super excited to have another SUV—and because the Yukon is cooler. Minivans feel like "mom haulers." The Odyssey and the Yukon both fit our family, but a deeper purpose than transportation motivated the purchase of each.

In the same way, every business exists for a basic purpose: to make money. But the best businesses have a deeper reason for existence that energizes the company. The best companies understand what that purpose is, and they use it to fuel their success.

Leveraging your company's purpose requires three steps. Number one, knowing why having a deep purpose is important. Number two, understanding how to craft and express that purpose. And number three, knowing how to use that purpose in your daily decisions. Let's look at each step.

Why Is Deep Purpose Important?

Think about one of the first questions you asked when you were young. If you can't remember, think about the first questions your kids asked. I bet that first question started with *why*. Because kids are curious and they want to understand the world. That desire for purpose is embedded in human nature.

A small child asks why to find meaning. That's also why having a deep purpose for your business is important. You must be able to define your business and understand how it should operate. That requires tapping into its deep meaning to you. Having a purpose is how you get skin in the game. Define your purpose so that it's ready to use when you need it.

Think about the construction business. It's risky, difficult, and competitive. Success requires dedication. Having a deep sense of purpose can guide you through the most difficult situations.

Deep purpose also keeps you from a life of regret. If you're just going through the motions in your business, you're setting yourself up for regrets. A deep sense of purpose can spare you that fate. It helps you understand how you're unique compared to other contractors and how that uniqueness can benefit your clients. It also safeguards you against greed.

A deep sense of purpose helps define and articulate your strategy and operations. It separates the great companies from the OK ones.

Purpose also leads to fulfillment. Every business solves problems and adds value, otherwise folks wouldn't give them money. But having a sense of purpose and acting on it results in a real sense of fulfillment. And the clearer your sense of purpose is, the more satisfying that sense of fulfillment.

Having a sense of deep purpose enables your business to make the contribution it's designed for. But how do you craft it?

How Do You Craft Your Deep Purpose?

Having skin in the game means accepting the risk related to your decisions. Not having skin in the game keeps you from caring about those decisions. Now think about the risks you've taken by owning a construction company. Do you accept responsibility for them?

When crafting your business's deep purpose, gather your core team. Whether it's just you and your business partner, a few investors, or a group of senior executives, make sure you all have skin in the game.

You may want to bring in a facilitator. If you're the leader of the company, facilitators always give you time to think. The best facilitators are able to synthesize the group's ideas into one or two key thoughts. And they make sure your vision isn't lost in the crowd.

Whether or not you get a facilitator, make sure to set aside adequate time. Finding your company's deeper purpose can take hours or days, depending on how vigorous and honest your team discussion is. So as you kick it off, recall what drove you to start your business.

I know what drove me to start mine: freedom and fun. In my business, I want freedom of time, association, and finance. I want to enjoy my work.

Don't be afraid to be idealistic. Think back to when you started, and ask your team these questions: "What's the purpose of our company? Why do we exist? What energizes us and gets us going?"

The first answer most people will come up with is this: "To make money." Fair enough, but ask them, "Why do we want to make money? Why are we in this particular business?" Keep asking why until you get to the core. Go beyond money and look for contribution and fulfillment.

Deeper purpose can be hard to articulate. But it must be authentic. Don't treat defining it as a marketing exercise. And don't worry about what other people think. I don't go around telling my clients that I'm in business for freedom and fun. But I keep it in my mind all the time to drive how I do business and who I do business with.

So avoid corporatese. Put it in your own words. You're not there to make other stakeholders feel good. A good purpose will attract some people, but it will repel others.

Articulating your deep sense of purpose is not a democratic process. You can receive feedback from your people who have skin in the game. But as the owner, you make the call about how to frame that deep sense of purpose. Let people weigh in so that they can buy in. But if something doesn't ring true, don't force it just to appease others.

Define your purpose authentically. And make sure to align your policies and procedures, who you hire, and who you fire around that purpose.

Then ask yourself, "Do I like my purpose statement? Does it sound like me, or does it sound fake and corporate?"

If it's not genuine, then go back through the process of finding your deeper purpose. Or if you have an authentic purpose, but you're not living by it, then recommit to it. Get your key stakeholders in the room and say, "Listen, guys. We haven't been living out our purpose. But we are going to do that from now on."

If that means you have to move some people out of your business, change some policies, or lose some customers, do it.

Allow your deeper purpose to drive your business.

You don't need to understand this deep sense of purpose to have a business. Plenty of businesses don't. But my conviction is that most of the excellent businesses know the deeper purpose that's driving them. And they use it to spark real success in their organizations.

Let me give you some examples of purpose statements from real-life construction companies. We'll kick it off with a framing company I know. Their purpose statement is "We exist to provide and endure."

One fire sprinkler contractor has the purpose statement "Building lives by saving lives."

And an air-conditioning company I know has the stated purpose "Making people's lives comfortable."

Notice how none of those statements are the same. But they're all rather personal. And there's a real sense of pride behind each one. Some of them, like the air-conditioning company and the sprinkler company, are industry-specific. The framing company wants the business to endure over many generations.

With those examples in mind, craft a purpose statement that holds unique personal significance. Then read on to learn how to use it.

How to Use Deep Purpose in Your Daily Decisions

The purpose of Nike is to crush Adidas. Competitiveness drives their organization. Defining their deeper purpose helps them decide who to hire, who to retain, and who to fire. It can do the same for you.

Amazon is another hard-core company. Jeff Bezos comes off as a goofy guy. But beneath his nerdy exterior, he's a hard-core dude. And it's demonstrated in how he runs his business. Unless you're a hard-core, driven person, you're not going to succeed at Amazon.

Nordstrom is another example. I broke a pair of sunglasses I bought there, and Nordstrom replaced them, no questions asked. Their purpose is to take care of their customers, and that drives their policies.

Now consider Apple. Their obsession with quality informs their design and manufacturing processes.

If you have a deep sense of purpose, it affects the people who work for you. It influences how you structure your policies. It can even affect your customers.

Purpose can drive your strategy as well. Which jobs you pick, which locations you work in, which clients you work for. All these are practical examples of how to use deep purpose in your daily decisions.

Deep purpose is a filter. When you're faced with a decision, ask yourself, "Is this decision in alignment with my purpose?" If it's not, don't do it.

Right now you might be thinking, *I don't need a purpose other than making money.*

Fair enough. I know how hard it is to make money, and if someone's writing you checks in a legitimate business, it's because you are solving their problems or adding value.

But for most people, making money isn't enough. The majority of people need a reason to keep going when the going's hard.

Because it's all about people, and there are as many different personalities as there are individuals. Here's how to factor that in.

Personality

There are 7.8 billion people in the world. We share much in common despite being unique individuals.

The Greeks proposed four fundamental personality types: sanguine, melancholic, phlegmatic, and choleric. Sanguine folks tend to be talkative, enthusiastic, active, and social. Melancholic people are introverted, analytical, detail oriented, and deep thinkers and feelers. Phlegmatic people are relaxed, quiet, easygoing, and caring, yet they often try to hide their emotions. Choleric people tend to be extroverted, independent, decisive, goal oriented, and ambitious.

The Greeks believed people had one or two primary temperaments. But most people's personalities contain all four temperaments to some degree.

The construction industry has more than 680,000 employers in the United States alone. All of those companies have much in common. They all bid on, plan for, execute, and try to get paid for work. Just like individuals, companies have unique personalities.

This section will explore how to discover your company's unique personality, how to clarify it, and how to use it as a competitive advantage. And we'll discuss how personality works with purpose to provide a solid foundation to drive your company's success.

What Is Personality?

I want to define personality and make a distinction between values and personality. What do we mean by personality? It's a characteristic way of thinking and behaving most clearly expressed in interactions with others. Personality includes behavioral characteristics that distinguish one company from another.

Let's talk about the difference between values and personality.

I think of values as table stakes. These are the principles and standards of behavior you must display to run a successful business. Almost every construction company I know values safety, quality, integrity, customer service, teamwork, and innovation.

The problem is that many people don't discuss values in enough detail. They don't talk about how their company is unique in personality terms.

Also keep in mind that companies have unique personalities just like individuals. A company's personality reflects the people who started, run, and work in it. So personality is more distinctive than value alone. It's meaningful to you, gives you a real sense of direction, and helps you understand how to build a successful company.

It's vital to have your personality and your purpose aligned. Because they form the foundation of any successful company. Purpose answers the question, "Why do we exist?" Personality answers the question, "How do we behave?"

Next we'll talk about how to discover and clarify your company's unique personality, how to use that personality as a competitive advantage, and how personality works with purpose to drive your company's ongoing success.

How to Discover and Clarify Your Unique Personality

Think about your best employee. Make a list of that person's behaviors. And if more than one person pops into your mind, list both. Consider what makes them the best. What specific behaviors are unique to them? How do they treat your clients? How do they interact with employees and project partners?

Shooting video is a cornerstone of my business. I work with a company called Splasheo that edits my videos. Their customer service is excellent. I was asking Gideon, Splasheo's founder, what motivates that customer service. Gideon is obsessed with taking care of his clients. It's just part of his personality.

Your best employees may not even be conscious of their behaviors. Thinking about what they do helps you codify unique behaviors that make your business successful. The more specific and descriptive you are, the better. For instance, answering on the first ring and replying to messages within twenty-four hours are positive customer service behaviors.

Then look at someone who is no longer with your organization. What characterizes someone who's not a good fit for your business? Asking this question is vital, because one issue a lot of construction companies struggle with is having people who may be technically sound but whose personalities clash with the company culture.

Here's an example. I worked for a close friend many years ago. He's a great guy who's built two successful businesses. But he is never on time. If one of your values is punctuality, this person would not fit into your organization.

Look at the people who fit your company best and then contrast them with the people who don't. How do those qualities show up in the ways they behave? Let the answer influence how you craft your personality statements.

State these personality aspects in your own words. And describe them in terms of behavior. This helps you get to the root personality that makes your business succeed. As with purpose, avoid corporate speak. It's not about looking good to others. It's about understanding yourself.

The more you understand your behavior, the more successful and happy you'll be. Not only as an individual but also as a company.

Because personality can help you against the competition. Keep reading to learn how.

Personality as a Competitive Advantage

We've covered how to define your personality. Now let's look at how to use your personality as a competitive advantage. And we're not just talking about marketing. We're talking about understanding yourself so that you can leverage that knowledge to stand out from the competition.

Lacking strategic clarity, employing workers who don't fit, and having annoying customers makes business hard. All these problems can be addressed if you understand and stay true to your personality. When you understand your personality, you understand your strengths and weaknesses. And you can take advantage of opportunities and avoid threats based on that understanding.

Think about the types of projects you like to build. Perhaps certain people in your organization influence which projects you build. Maybe you're committed to a certain industry, like health care. Or maybe you just love moving dirt.

Look at what you value, choose how you behave, and act accordingly. Maybe you're adept at playing the corporate game; therefore, you go after corporate opportunities. Or perhaps you're a bit of a cowboy, and you want to build for cowboys. You could be the type of person who loves to negotiate, and you like complicated projects you can haggle over.

Then think about where you build. Maybe you want to work in an urban environment and be involved in high-profile projects. On the other hand, you may be content in a less dense, more low-key environment. It all depends on the personality of your organization.

If you understand the personality of your company, you will begin to attract the right people and repel the wrong people. You should be embedding personality questions into your interviewing process. You want as many people who line up with your company's personality as possible. So weed out people whose personalities don't fit. That way, you can better integrate personality with purpose.

How Personality Integrates with Purpose

Aligning personality and purpose is like building your company on rock. Companies whose purpose and personality are misaligned are built on sand. And when the storms of business come, they're plunged into chaos. But the companies with a strong foundation of personality and purpose withstand, and even thrive in, those storms.

Purpose and personality determine everything your company does from a planning and execution perspective. If you're clear on your purpose and personality, you can use them as filters. When you're deciding on opportunities, hiring, and setting policies and procedures, ask yourself, "Does this further the purpose of our company in alignment with our personality?"

Remember the framing company? Their purpose is "We exist to provide and endure." They further state their personality as "The courage to break molds and eliminate excuses. The discipline to kick ass. The wisdom to stay humble together."

That may appeal to you; it may not. But it's a true reflection of the core of their organization and why they have been successful.

Have you ever taken a personality test? If so, I bet it helped you understand yourself more. Maybe you leveraged that knowledge to help you be more successful. Take the opportunity to do the same for your business. Then communicate your personality starting with your people.

To guide decisions in your organization, your personality must align with your strategic plan. Let's examine how.

Plan

We've talked about purpose and personality. Now we need to discuss your plan.

What's a plan? It's your answer to the question, "How are we going to succeed?"

Are you crystal clear on how you will succeed? Most companies are fuzzy on it. Of course, if your business is making money, you do have some idea of how you're succeeding. But the companies that are crystal clear on how to succeed experience healthy growth and robust profitability year after year.

The first step to success is nailing your niche, or niches, if you have more than one. That means having the right client and the right job in the right location.

The second step is to be clear about your edge. What sets you apart from your many competitors? Leveraging your edge could mean giving detailed, accurate estimates. Or staying on budget better than anyone else.

If you don't have an edge, it means there are some areas you need to work on. Make a list of your strengths and weaknesses. Then do a strengths, weaknesses, opportunities, and threats (SWOT) analysis.

What was the last project you kicked some ass on? Why did you excel at it? Team ownership? Lateral thinking? Good bid focus? Pin it down.

Now let's look at the other side of the coin. What was the last project that fell through? Why did it fail? Lack of teamwork and technical expertise? Poor communication? Bad management?

It's crucial that you answer these questions to plan for success on a strategic and project basis.

One of my subcontractor clients wants to gross 22 percent and net a 12 percent minimum on every project. They've got a strategic plan articulated to support the field and the shop. So they promote and develop from within. That's how they state their mission and let it guide them.

Your purpose and personality won't change much over time. But your plan will change with the market. And when the plan changes, you need to know what to address first. That's where priority comes in.

Priority

"What is most important right now?" The answer will help you set priorities and achieve your rally cry.

We discussed the rally cry before. The right one can shift team focus to your priorities. Those priorities will inform the larger plan, which will be guided by your purpose and personality.

Now ask yourself, "Does our leadership team understand our rally cry? Have they bought into it? Are they communicating it to everyone in our organization?"

To review so far, here are the four Ps: purpose, personality, plan, priority. It's vital to be able to communicate them to your team. Next, I'll teach you how.

The Power of Communicating Your Company's Values Every Day

The purpose and personality of a company is most often in the heart and mind of its founders. It's expressed in the company's behavior, but it's not always articulated clearly. And that's a huge missed opportunity to gain good collaborators.

Write out your personality and purpose. Make it clear and personal. Then share it. By sharing it, you're defining your company's culture. When someone acts counter to it, you can call it out. That eases accountability. Your workers don't have to guess what you want them to do. They just align themselves with the organization's purpose and personality.

They can even get involved in helping meet your purpose and personality in deeper ways. Invite your employees to share their ideas about how to steer the company in even better directions.

Making your company's purpose and personality explicit also makes it simpler to hire and fire. Use them as conditions of employment. "Stick to these personality behaviors, and we'll be golden. Deviate from them, and we're done." Simplify your life, and give your team clarity on whether they belong with you or not.

Build your purpose and personality into everything you do. Make them part of every workday. That way they can guide your business to achieve more than just maximizing profit, which can take you to dangerous places. Purpose and personality will guide you toward greener pastures instead of danger.

Lead Your Company from the Front

Let's review.

- Purpose: "Why does our company exist?"
- Personality: "How does our company behave?"
- Plan: "How are we going to succeed?"
- Priority: "What's most important right now?"

These four concepts help generate employee buy-in, because they're about more than just money. They're personal.

COVID-19 and other global issues have caused delays and pressures. Thus, removing confusion, disorder, and lack of progress in your organization is critical. The four Ps can bring clarification, align your people with your purpose, and drive progress.

Confirm that all your employees are on the same page and that they'll hold you to the same standard. So live your purpose and personality, and communicate the plan.

This will feed into the legacy you want to leave, which we'll talk about next.

CHAPTER 9

LEGACY: THE NEXT GENERATION, SUCCESSION PLANS, AND SELLING THE COMPANY

Do you have a succession plan?

If you own a construction company, you don't want to just shut it down when you retire. You want to pass it on to someone who cares about it as much as you do. A major challenge many construction companies face is when their succession plan fails.

Why do succession plans fail so often? About half the people who sell their businesses are dissatisfied with them. Many people reach the end of a business venture only to find it wasn't as fulfilling as they were led to believe it would be. They just want out. Now.

Our innate desire to leave behind a legacy feeds that frustration. Business owners want to sell, but they want some input into the company's future. They also want financial independence. From this emotional state, they pick their successors based on their feelings about the company, not what's best for the company. They micromanage the transfer until their successors get discouraged. When the dust settles, the company ends up in the hands of someone who wasn't their first choice.

Business owners often appraise their own companies' worth far above market value. It's hard to be objective after investing forty years into a business.

So how do you avoid these pitfalls when you're ready to retire? I'm here to help you navigate this minefield. Let's discuss how you can structure your business for successful succession from day one.

Getting Legacy Right

Good succession planning is good strategic planning. You can build your company with succession in mind from the beginning. If you didn't do that, it's not too late to start.

What's your number one postretirement goal? Do you want continued jobs for your former workers? A legacy with your name on it? A maximum payout? How do you want to run your company, and how do you want it to run after you retire?

If you're a sole owner who never took on partners, you may want to hand the company over to another single owner. If you're in a group of owners, you might be able to entrust it to a longtime partner. The way you run your business determines a lot about how you can hand it off.

It's important to keep a realistic evaluation of what your business is worth. I recommend getting your business appraised by a third party (i.e., a professional business appraiser) every two to three years to keep your perspective clear. Some business owners get within a few years of retirement and expect to make $20 million from the sale. In reality, they're lucky to get one-tenth of that.

Another harsh reality to keep in mind is that two-thirds of construction companies are unsaleable. What makes a company unsellable? When the barriers to entry are too low. That is, when it's better to build a start-up than to buy an existing business. Existing businesses are harder to fix when they're broken, whereas a start-up can be planned and built right from day one. After all, anyone can open an office and call themselves a construction company. Why buy one when you can just start one? Construction leaders have a hard time stomaching this, so it bears repeating for emphasis: many buyers don't want the hassle of dealing with someone else's below-average business practices when they can design one themselves from the ground up.

For this reason, third-party sales are hard to secure. Other succession avenues bear much better fruit, and it's a good idea to explore them.

Another difficulty in selling a construction company is that owners are often involved in the day-to-day operations. They're not just selling a business but a job that needs doing, too. That's a bitter pill for prospective buyers to swallow, and few are willing to cough up $10 million for a demanding job.

So what makes a construction company desirable to a buyer? The biggest factor is the owners being uninvolved in any of the daily tasks. This way the owner can step out, and the business runs itself. Nothing about the company would change with the transition of owners because it manages itself. This sort of system also tends to create a much higher valuation of the company. This is the kind of value that's hard to build. A multimillion-dollar company that runs itself with little required input from the owner is the ideal offer that attracts the best buyers.

This also means setting up your company to seek repeat revenue so that there's a predictable stream of income. If the owner has to track down new customers or wonders when clients will show up, that's a turnoff. Constant repeat business is worth paying for.

Once you've identified what you want your succession to look like, and what you can realistically expect, let's look at your options. Think about managing your emotions and making the choice that best fulfills your succession goals. Identify how long it will take to transition your business when the time comes. It doesn't happen overnight. Who will take over which aspects of your job, from daily activities to occasional priorities that still need to get done? If that's unclear, you don't own a business—you own a day job. Fix that immediately, or you don't have a sellable company.

Even if the thought of retirement is twenty years away, think about hiring an appraiser and talking to a business broker who can help you keep realistic expectations. A clear vision grounded in reality, not feelings, is what keeps surprises to a minimum.

When to Begin the Succession Process

I said before that the best time to start planning for succession is on day one. The second best time is today. But you can't just close your eyes and wait for the big picture to appear. That picture needs to align with the reality of where your business is. Build along the path of that picture to design your business around the transition.

Is that to say you'll never get lucky? Or that you can't sell your business in a year if you haven't planned for it? Not at all. Lots of business deals are made every day. But remember, you're aiming to be the one construction business owner out of six who doesn't regret selling. By planning now, you're hedging your bets. The more advanced notice you have, the better your odds.

Many business owners think, *I've invested so much of myself in this business, it's a reflection of me. I know how awesome it is.* So they tie up their egos in the process. They don't want to think about the succession plan early because it feels like they're giving up on their life's work.

Planning when the weather is good is the best time to do so. Something could take you out of the business before you intend to leave. You could get cancer. Or get into an accident. You may have to make a cross-country move unexpectedly. If any of those situations happen, you'll be glad you had an exit plan already in the works.

Many of our decisions are based on narratives we have in our minds. Every business has ups and downs, and so do our lives. In transition planning, think through the worst-case scenarios so that you don't get blindsided by circumstances beyond your control.

Who Should Help You Plan?

Consider who you should involve in transition planning to maximize your success. If you're married, your spouse's expectations need to be addressed. You also need some professionals: your accountant, an appraiser, a business broker, and a business lawyer who understands the process.

It might be tempting to bring in your whole trusted staff. But too many cooks can spoil the broth. You and your spouse, any partners, and the professionals who can provide crucial data and expertise are enough. Anyone else on whom the decision has a direct impact, such as a successor in or out of your family, can be included.

When to Unveil Your Succession Plan

Some people wait until the last possible second to name a successor. Think of kings who've done this in the past. It doesn't go well.

Your people need a chance to adjust. If you wait until you're on your deathbed, you'll shock your whole company. And you might not get a chance to announce a successor at all!

What will your employees think if you're seventy years old and you still haven't named a successor? Or say you're sixty and end up in the hospital. Suddenly everyone is afraid, not only for your health but also for their jobs. They may start thinking about changing jobs just to give themselves some peace of mind. Failing to declare a succession plan can cost you your best employees.

When to unveil your plan is a personal decision. But let me encourage you to reveal it at the first sign of company anxiety over your age or health. Provide your people with the security of knowing who's next in line. Make sure you give them time to adjust to the idea of a new owner. Some owners announce they're selling the company a month before the sale finalizes. That's terrifying for employees.

You don't have to get everything perfect before you announce, either. Just give people an idea of what would happen if you were out and how long they can expect to work with you. That assurance will go a long way for everyone.

How to Make Your Company Attractive for a Potential Buyer

Would you pay $10 million for a sixty-hour-per-week job? Of course not. That's why, as I mentioned before, taking yourself out of day-to-day operations is the best thing you can do. To make this happen, you need to build processes.

Automate as much of your business as possible by delegating tasks to your management team. By building a company that can run without you, you'll overcome one of the biggest hurdles to selling or transferring your business. Because you won't be passing on a job. You'll be handing over an asset.

This will also improve your quality of life. Imagine working a few hours a day and making just as much money as you do now. What would you do with all that extra time? You could even start a second business and double your income. All because you prepped for succession and automated your company by delegating tasks.

Plus, you'll have better odds of avoiding the biggest company transfer issues, such as . . .

The Biggest Transfer Issues

Hands down, letting go of control is the hardest part of the transition process. To many business owners, handing over a company they founded to someone else is like losing a part of themselves.

For a lot of us, being a business owner is our whole identity. Who are we without our companies? And what happens if they don't reflect us anymore? If a new owner makes too many changes, it can feel like a betrayal. So we bottleneck the succession process out of fear.

Do you insist on controlling every part of your company? Demanding that the new owner must run things your way is a guaranteed bad sale. The new owner may back out if you're too overbearing.

If you want a smooth transfer process, be ready to let go. Don't invest so much of yourself in being a business owner that you forget you can be anything else. And get your management team making some of their own decisions so that you can release some of that workload. This will all help during the transition to another owner. You won't feel the need to maintain total control.

But you will need a way to bring the new owner up to speed.

KPIs to Track

As a part of your succession plan, you need to track the key performance indicators (KPIs) of your business.

How do you do this? Start by recording a few metrics.

- Cost to completion
- Billing accuracy
- Length of billing cycles
- Turnover rate

These key factors can give you a snapshot of how your business is doing. New owners will want to see these metrics. So will potential buyers. No matter how you move through succession, you'll need to account for the state of your business to know what your successor is taking on.

If you don't know these KPIs now, you're not running a business. You're coasting along hoping it's working out. Get a smart accountant and building systems that measure your workforce to track these indicators ruthlessly. The more data you have, the better. That's true for succession, sales, and daily business operations.

Because your metrics tell a story. They show how your business has grown over the years. Or how it hasn't. They also show what your customers expect, the quality of your talent pool, and the strength of your management team.

When people ask, "Why shouldn't I just start my own construction business?" you can pull out your KPIs to show them they won't be able to build a system that efficient or that profitable.

Your KPIs are your selling point. They also show you where to improve, even if you plan to stay in business for another twenty years.

Start tracking KPIs now. When you're ready to sell, you'll have that much more data to prove your company's value.

Immediate Steps to Take That Will Benefit You Later

Let's say you're three to five years away from retirement. And you think it's too late to set up your business for succession. Let me reassure you, it's not too late. You've still got great options on the table. It's all about what you do next.

First, start tracking your KPIs. Get as many years of those metrics as you can. They will serve you well as you figure out which direction to move in going forward. And when you do succeed or sell, you can hand over those metrics as proof of value.

Second, get out of the office. Start automating. Delegate decisions. Build processes. Keep doing more and more to put yourself out of a job. If you do this for the next several months, you'll find yourself with extra time on your hands. That's good, because you'll be able to relax. And you can attract a buyer who wants an asset, not a job.

Last but not least, focus on relationships. At the end of your career, it won't be about how many projects you finished or how much money you made but the quality of your relationships. Those relationships will help lead you to the best successor or buyer, too. Sometimes your dream buyer is someone you've done business with for years. Don't neglect your relationships, because they'll carry the day in the end.

Don't worry about doing everything flawlessly. No business looks perfect to any buyer. The key is lining up all the pieces you can to maximize your company's value and boost its attractiveness to the next owner.

Following these three steps will optimize your chance of selling your business and feeling good about it. And you'll make your life better in the meantime. Because you'll be able to relax knowing you've streamlined your company.

Win now, and win later. That's the best approach to succession plans and business sales.

In the next chapter, we'll discuss how company priorities will help you achieve your long-term business plans.

CHAPTER 10

SETTING COMPANY PRIORITIES STRAIGHT

In chapter 8, we introduced you to priority, the most important thing you must communicate to your company. Your priority may change every thirty, sixty, or ninety days. And that makes sense when you understand why.

You remember the other three Ps, of course. Well, your priority is always rooted in your purpose and personality. They never change. The plan flows from those two unchanging parts of you. And your priority shifts as you move through the stages of your plan. A plan might change every one to five years depending on how it's structured. Your current priority is just the next step of that plan.

Changing priority just means taking the next step. That makes you easy to follow. Three years from now, you might be pursuing different projects at different locations. But your purpose and personality will be the same, your plan will flow from those, and your priority will flow from the plan.

Priority is the moving piece, the leverage you control to make your plan happen. That's why priority gets its own chapter. It's smart to figure out your personality and purpose, and it's wise to draw up a plan. But if you don't leverage your short time windows to accomplish that plan, it's all for nothing. Priority is where the rubber meets the road. And it's where you live day-to-day.

Most people don't understand priority. They think it's about short-term goals that make them feel good. Sometimes they're just treading water. Or they don't know how to motivate their teams to attack the same priority. In this chapter, I'll show you how to focus on your short-term future to accomplish your long-term goals and motivate your team to join you on your mission.

Priority

Advances in warfare in the late eighteenth century produced great numbers of injuries and casualties. People saw a need for more efficient caregiving to wounded soldiers on the battlefield.

In 1792, Baron Dominique Jean Larrey, a French doctor who would later serve as surgeon in chief to Napoleon's Imperial Guard, first implemented what would become known as the triage system.

Dr. Larrey's system filtered injured soldiers into three groups: dangerously wounded, less dangerously wounded, and slightly wounded. The worse the injury, the higher the treatment priority. Larrey's methods not only saved soldiers' lives but also boosted troop morale. His strict triage rules, based on severity of condition and likelihood of recovery, ignored rank and nationality. The triage system saved Larrey, too, in an unexpected manner.

After the Battle of Waterloo, Larrey was wounded and captured by the Prussians. He was quite close to Napoleon, and the Battle of Waterloo was the end of Napoleon's reign. Which should have meant the end of Larrey's life.

Larrey was about to be shot when the Prussian soldier tying the blindfold recognized him. Instead of being executed, Larrey was sent to Prussian General von Blücher. Larrey had saved von Blücher's son's life after a previous battle, so von Blücher invited him to dine with his family. After dinner, Larrey was released with money and a military escort. His idea of treating the wounded, regardless of rank or nationality, saved his life.

In a time of crisis, when resources are limited and time is of the essence, it's important for medical facilities to prioritize who they treat. In the same way, you have limited time and resources. You need to identify your top priority. That means learning to look at the issues your construction business faces. Which are the most important right now? What initiatives can you undertake to address them?

Your top priority needs to be simple. That's why I'll teach you a step-by-step method for identifying your most important priority and building a simple action plan to execute it. We'll start by asking three questions. First, what is a priority? Second, how do you identify and clarify your priorities? And third, how do you build an action plan around your priority?

What Is a Priority?

To reiterate, your top priority answers the question, "What's most important right now?" You also have to define "right now."

In my experience, a ninety-day priority hits the sweet spot. It gives you enough time to get real work done, it doesn't rush you too much, and it lets you balance your priorities with your overall strategic plan.

A strategic plan may last from one to three years. But again, your priority should be based on a thirty-, sixty-, or ninety-day cycle, with ninety days being the best in my opinion.

Why is prioritization important? You have to prioritize in business for the same reasons doctors prioritize in triage. You have limited time, money, and manpower. Those resources must be marshaled and focused on what's most important at the time.

Human beings thrive when they can concentrate. We do not multitask well. In fact, a study from the University of London found that multitasking impairs IQ as much as smoking a joint. If you want your company to perform as if you and your employees are stoned, then continue to multitask.

You can't do everything. Nor should you try to. You should spend time figuring out what's most important right now and executing on that. Companies that excel at identifying their priorities enjoy unity in their organization as a result. The best leaders can rally their troops around a specific outcome to generate momentum, accountability, and a sense of accomplishment.

And picking one priority to focus on provides useful feedback. You can see what happens as a result of your action. You may have to adjust your priority or your plan. But without that focus, it's hard to figure out whether you're making progress. Prioritization gives you that focus.

Next, we'll focus on clarity.

How to Identify and Clarify Priorities

You identify and clarify through a combination of numbers and conversations.

Let's talk about your construction business. Your business has three main areas. You bid work, you build work, and you bill work. Each area has associated numbers. With bidding, you can measure hit rate and repeat customers. When it comes to building, you can clarify and identify metrics from your schedule and other aspects of your business. As far as billing is concerned, you can look at outstanding accounts receivable or under- and overbillings.

But numbers tell only part of the story. They direct you where conversations need to happen. The numbers are the skeleton on which you hang flesh and skin via conversation. Together they guide you in making necessary choices.

The art of leadership is all about the quality of the choices you make. As a leader in your construction company, you must be able to talk with your team, identify what's most important right now, and execute it.

If you aren't tracking metrics, start. Delegate the task to someone whose job it should be anyway. Collect the numbers. Then put them up on the wall and look at them. What story do the numbers tell? Where are you weak? Where are you strong?

Then converse with your team. Are the metrics bad? Get curious with problem-solving. Don't assume bad actors at work right off the bat. No one is sabotaging your business. So what are you missing? What insights can your team share that give you the complete picture?

Once you've got the picture, now you can plant your flag.

Plant Your Flag, Call Your Shot, Set Your Priority

Sometimes the many demands of your business make it hard to prioritize. But this process is crucial to accomplishing your goals. And it can be used in all parts of your organization.

In the best businesses, the senior executive team can stand above the fray and see which part of the business needs attention. It's important for the company that they work as a team and not demand action in an area that would harm the overall strategy.

In response to some of the challenges posed by COVID-19, one of my clients shifted resources from project management into their estimating department. That way they could generate more sales to replenish their backlog. They were able to execute that pivot because both teams were flexible together.

Your job as the leader is to make decisions. You can't make everyone happy all the time. You have the final word on what's most important right now. That may ruffle some feathers. But you do a disservice to all of your people when you don't make a decision. The best leaders are willing to bear the burden of making others unhappy to benefit the organization. And the best executive teams are willing to commit to the leader's decision in spite of disagreement.

Many years ago, one of my clients was struggling with underbillings. Their project managers weren't focused on getting bills out to clients. So the clients couldn't pay, and the cash didn't flow. The gentleman in charge of accounting informed the senior executive team of the situation. They all agreed to work with the project management team to make sure that completed work was billed for. Cash flow shifted to positive. Their focus made all the difference.

Focusing on priorities can save your business, too. Clarify what matters right now and address it as a team. Build action plans with a rally cry, areas of fierce focus, and critical numbers. That's how you accomplish your goals.

I encourage you to get with your team and identify your most pressing priority. What's most important right now? What must you get done in the next ninety days to make real progress? Download the one-page template from my website, and use it to direct your plan and priority meeting.

PART 3:
CONSTRUCTION SALES AND MARKETING

CHAPTER 11

SALES: KNOW, LIKE, TRUST, BUY

In a good economy, there is plenty of construction work to go around, and it keeps everyone busy. We've seen periods like this over the last twenty years. They come. And go.

It's the lean times—like the one many entrepreneurs see coming at the time of this writing—that separate the owners from the hobbyists. When it's hard to find work, how do you make the sale? Success comes down to strategy—the strategy I'm about to teach you.

In this chapter, we will take the time to understand the psychology behind selling and buying. Because sales struggles are not about sales; they're about people. To that end, this chapter will explore the human side of the sale so that you can close more of them for higher amounts—even when everyone around you is fumbling for business.

Meta Sales Tip: Identify the Final Decision Maker

Nothing you learn about sales will be useful if you're deploying that knowledge in conversations with the wrong people. Underperforming salespeople do just that. But not you and your team.

Quick story—I was talking to a contractor some time ago. They were bidding on an $80 million project, which for them was considerable. I asked them, "Who's the final decision maker at that company? In other words, who's the person who'll be signing the contract to engage your construction services?"

What do you think their answer was? Keep in mind, this was an $80 million project. They poured a ton of blood, sweat, and tears into getting their proposal just right.

"I don't know."

Think about the times you were going after a project, and you had no idea who the final decision maker was. Now think about the last time you lost a sale. Were you crystal clear on who was influencing the decision for that particular sale? Or who would be signing the contract? And who had the final decision maker's ear? These factors go hand in hand. If you don't know who (and what) influences whether you get the job, it's doubtful you'll close the sale when times are hard.

Every sales objective has a unique set of influences. You may know who would approve a $10 million project, but a $50 million project may be overseen by someone completely different. Identify the influences on each project, and you'll maximize your chances of courting them, getting their buy-in, and closing the sale.

The Four Buyers You Need to Know

In any sale in the construction industry, there are four main buyers you'll interact with, a fact I learned from the business classic *Strategic Selling* by Robert B. Miller and Stephen E. Heiman. Let's discuss each one and learn how you can approach them for maximum success.

The Economic Buyer

The economic buyer is your final decision maker. There's always one person giving the final approval for any given sale. Even if there's a decision-making committee, there's always a leader. This economic buyer can say yes when everybody else says no and can veto a deal that everybody else approves.

What defines an economic buyer? Besides having spending authority and veto power, the economic buyer is focused on the bottom line and what impact the ROI will have on the organization.

The User Buyer

The role of the user buyer is to make judgments about your construction services' impact on job performance. A user buyer could be the general contractor's superintendent or the construction manager who's representing the owner. If you're a general contractor, your user buyer could be an architect or an engineer. User buyers use or supervise the use of your service. And their personal success is tied to the success of your work for them. There may be several people playing the user buyer role in a sale.

The user buyer's focus is on the job to be done. They're asking, "How will it help me do my job?"

The Technical Buyer

The technical buyer is a gatekeeper focused on the service itself. They're looking at how well you can meet a variety of objective specifications. Technical buyers can't give a final yes, but they can say no. Technical buyers sometimes present themselves as the final decision maker, even though they never are.

The task of the technical buyer is to narrow down the list of sellers and come up with a shorter list for the economic buyer. They don't decide who wins, but they do decide who gets to play the game. They focus on matching specifications in their area of expertise. Technical buyers ask, "Does this company meet my specifications?"

The Coach Buyer

The coach buyer guides the contractor to the other buyers and gives necessary information for effective sales positioning with each one. They're the one rooting for your company to close the sale, and they want to help you. Coaches can be found inside or outside the buying organization, even inside your own.

Coaches can give information about your bid's validity, identify other buying influences, and offer advice on strategy.

The Buying Influences Chart: How Buyers Fit Together

There's a systematic way of identifying the buying influencers for each sale you pursue. We start by creating a buying influences chart.

Buying Influences Chart

Economic
Releases $$

User
Judges impact on job

Technical
Screens out

Coach(es)
Guides me on **this** sale

For each sale you go after, start a new chart. Open a document and begin by writing down the economic buyer, the user buyer, the technical buyer, and the coach. Fill in the names of the people in each role. This is how you'll track everyone important to the sale and what you're doing to address them.

Next, identify any red flags that jeopardize your chances of winning this job. The first automatic red flag is missing information that you've been unable to get. This includes uncertainty about specs, buying influencers who don't return your emails, and any buying influencers who are new to the organization.

Your coach buyer could be one of your red flags. How can you go after the job if you can't get the information you need? But if the information is missing only on your side, you can find a new coach to help you fill in those gaps. The best coach is the one who can fill in the most information gaps for you. That's why I said coaches can be in the other organization or your own. Whoever eliminates this red flag is the coach you want.

Red flags vary for each type of buyer, too.

The economic buyer needs to be addressed based on ROI. It's not about offering the best price (unless you are in a hard-bid environment). It's about giving the best return on investment. So what can be expected in return for the expense of hiring you? How does your service help their whole company in the long run? If you don't know what you're offering, you might not make the sale. Identify how this project helps your client and how you can help them achieve it better than anyone else.

The user buyer wants to look good and wants work to flow smoothly. How does your service facilitate those outcomes? Excellent customer service from your front line is huge for the user buyer. Friction is your enemy. Any friction means the buyer needs to make excuses to the boss.

If there's a complication, you should be the first one offering solutions. Don't be the person who sits back twiddling their thumbs waiting for the client to tell you how to address the problem. Give them the best solution, and ask if they want you to proceed. Minimize their friction so that any complications are as small and painless as possible for them. That makes them look great for hiring you.

Technical buyers are forgotten a lot. But they're crucial. How are you addressing their concerns as they narrow down the list of candidates so that you're still in the running? It's not only about ROI or less friction but also about the best fit for their company. Can you deliver what they believe is necessary? Do you have the technical knowledge that tells them they won't find glaring oversights in the completed project?

If your niche is hospitals, take the time to learn about every need a hospital staff might have. Don't just build what you think a hospital should look like. You may need to interview staff at other locations in your niche and ask what they feel is missing or what they wish was added. Then you can suggest these things to your clients during the buying process to show your expertise. They'll trust you not to leave them with a building they regret.

The Psychology of Selling: Know, Like, Trust . . . Then Buy

I'd like to tell you a little love story. But it wasn't love at first sight.

I'm eight years older than my wife. We first met when she was a teenager and I was in my midtwenties. No, there were no romantic sparks. I saw her as a kid, and she thought of me as an old man. But as time passed, things began to change. We got to know each other. We knew, liked, and trusted each other. And that changed our relationship. After six years, we were married. My wife and I, at the time of this writing, will celebrate our twentieth anniversary next year in Hawaii with our five children.

No matter what we're buying, be it a business opportunity or a life-long relationship, people always prefer to purchase from those they know, like, and trust. If you're going to be successful in construction and selling, whether to owners, developers, or general contractors, people must get to know you before they commit to working with you.

Know

Let's look at three simple ways you can get to know a potential project partner, and vice versa.

1. Get your face in the place.
2. Drop the ego.
3. Persist.

One of my construction clients is an expert at getting his face in the place. He's the CEO and rainmaker of his company. He's willing to drive, fly, and spend the time getting to know potential clients. Yes, it takes time. But why not invest three hours into a project you're likely to get instead of an hour each into three projects you'll probably lose? Get out of the office, hit the road, and meet your buying influences in person. You'll learn so much more about them than you do talking on the phone. Showing up strengthens your potential project partners' confidence in you.

Now let's talk about ego.

During the early days of World War II, Britain faced the Nazi menace alone. Winston Churchill was the British prime minister, and he had a massive ego, but he was not a fool. He realized that defeat was likely without American support. So he expended a great deal of energy getting to know US President Franklin Delano Roosevelt.

Churchill didn't grovel, but he framed the situation in terms that appealed to America. He emphasized America's military and economic might and the responsibility and opportunity that came with that power. Churchill's goal was to get the US in the war, on his side against the Germans. He didn't try to make his relationship with Roosevelt all about Britain. He focused on what was in it for them. And that helped to strengthen the relationship between the two countries.

The construction services you provide solve problems and add value to your clients. When you're getting to know them, don't make it all about you. Like Churchill, drop the ego and focus on how *you* can benefit *them*.

There's much to be said for the power of persistence. What's the right response the first time you're rejected? It's not "OK, thank you. Have a nice day." Click. Instead, show up at their door and ask if they have any projects you can collaborate on. If they say no, visit them again the following week. And again. Keep persisting unless they blatantly ask you to stop.

I've been in sales for over thirty years, and I've learned that persistence pays off. Most of my success over the years has been due to persistence. I just kept showing up.

If you're searching for work, create a list of your top ten or twenty potential clients. Start showing up at their offices with a proactive, ego-free, problem-solving mindset. Use the buying influences chart to keep track of and take notes on everyone you speak to. (Review these notes before each visit. No one likes to feel forgotten or have to repeat themselves.) And commit to persisting until you win a project with them.

Like

Now the big question: How can you get people to like you? Once again, here are three ways:

1. Be an equal.
2. Be helpful.
3. Be yourself.

Remember the movie *Shrek*? Eddie Murphy voices the slightly insecure donkey, who's super anxious to win the friendship of the ogre Shrek. In time, Donkey and Shrek grow to like each other. But it wasn't because Donkey kissed up to Shrek.

When you're selling work to potential or existing clients, your goal is not to be subservient. Show up as an equal. All healthy relationships are based on mutual benefit and respect. Nobody likes a desperate, groveling salesperson. If you're holding your people accountable for business development, nobody has to be desperate. Focus on delivering excellent projects, and you'll land the right projects for your business. Delivering excellence includes being helpful.

How do you cultivate helpfulness? In the summer of 1997, I'd been put in charge of planning a multiday retreat for a volunteer organization I belonged to. I was nervous and uncomfortable about the whole thing.

Over fifty people were attending, which made for complicated logistics. I had a limited amount of time. I'm an expert at *facilitating* retreats. But planning them is not my strong suit. So the closer the retreat date came, the more stressed out I got.

That was when Mike stepped in. Mike was a younger volunteer who noticed my discomfort. He asked if I needed assistance. I didn't know him that well, but I soon found he was an expert event planner. He helped me organize and plan everything, and the retreat was a smashing success. It was the beginning of a friendship that's lasted over twenty years. He stepped up and helped me in my time of need. That's why I like Mike.

The best way to help your potential clients is to become an expert at uncovering their problems in the various phases of their projects. Identify your clients' needs and meet them. If you can offer them assistance in the same way Mike helped me, they'll like you immediately.

But . . . not everyone is going to like you. Neither will everyone want to do business with you. It's still vital to be yourself.

I was chatting with one of my clients recently. Like many senior construction executives, he oversees the bid, plan, and build portions of the business. We were discussing his approach to selling, and he said something that struck me.

"Some people like rib eye. Others just want a hamburger."

Both rib eye and hamburger come from cows, and they both fill up the stomach. Rib eyes are more expensive and supposedly tastier. But not everyone thinks so. Some people just prefer a good burger. My client's company is rib eye. He's come to accept that not everyone likes the way they approach projects. And that's OK.

Sales isn't about getting everyone to like you. It's about understanding yourself, your company, and the value you provide. Then you can get busy finding people who see and appreciate *that* value.

Think about your top ten to twenty clients. How many of them like you? You can work on developing that bond by helping them with a problem. Remember to show up as an equal. Kings talk to kings. Don't come in with a cheesy look on your face begging for work. Stay true to who you and your company are.

Not everyone is going to like you, and you don't need to win every project—just the right projects with the right people.

Trust (and Buy)

Did you kick off the New Year with some fresh resolutions? Maybe you pledged to hit the gym, avoid sweets, or cut down to one glass of wine instead of three.

Establishing healthy new routines isn't easy. A study in the *European Journal of Social Psychology* found that it takes sixty-six days on average to build a new routine. Not only that, but the length of time varies from person to person, ranging from eighteen to 154 days.

Just like it takes time and practice to build a new habit, it takes your potential clients time to trust you. Let's look at three practical ways construction executives can build trust.

1. Start small.
2. Be responsive.
3. Add value.

It's OK to start small. They don't all have to be home runs. For all his faults, Pete Rose, the all-time Major League Baseball hit leader, had 4,256 hits. Seventy-five percent of those hits were singles, with fewer than 4 percent being home runs. Even though Rose was not a home run hitter, he was extremely effective.

Construction has a unique combination of technical difficulty, compressed timelines, and risk. When you're first trying to establish a relationship with a new client, you won't be handed a massive job to bid. The first time you contact them, expect to start small, whatever that means for you. Be willing to budget, bid on, and build a small project so that you can get to know your project partner and develop familiarity.

Now think about the tons of emails stuffing your inbox. How long have they been sitting there? Time is not friendly to most construction projects. The more time that passes, the bigger the challenges get. This is why it's important to be responsive. Implement a twenty-four-hour rule to respond to all emails from clients or potential clients. Don't be one of those contractors who hides in the corner until it's time to get paid. Be out front, proactive, and available. Your clients will appreciate that they can count on you to add value.

Speaking of, how can you add value? The complexity of construction causes difficulties, but it also presents opportunities. When was the last time you value engineered a project and gave your client an alternative that benefited them? Savvy owners and contractors are looking for partners who care about all parties making money. Don't just throw numbers at a project you were asked to bid. Generate confidence in your capabilities by taking the time to dive into the plans and look for creative ways to solve problems. This is adding value.

The bad news about the trust-building stage of construction is that sometimes you get burned. A developer has been talking about a project that's right in your wheelhouse for five years. You've spent hours and dollars on preconstruction services. And the deal never happens. There's no way around it but to accept this adversity as part of the game. If you keep focusing on identifying the right clients and the right jobs, you'll get burned less often than your competitors do.

How much trust have you built with each of your top potential clients? What small jobs can you bid? Do you have any unanswered emails from them? How can you add value to them by helping to solve their problems? You'll begin to reap the rewards as you concentrate on building these working relationships.

The Five Salespeople You Employ without Realizing It

My house is always a mess. My wife and I work hard to involve our kids in cleaning up, but it's a challenge. Kids believe their job is to consume vast amounts of food, play *Fortnite* with their friends, and sleep. I'm half joking.

Just like my kids don't yet grasp their responsibility to help keep our home clean, some folks in your business development roles may not comprehend their essential responsibility. To help you clarify the situation for these individuals, I'll discuss five types of people who are most likely within your sales teams as well as simple ways to improve their performance. The five types are the following:

1. Enthusiasts
2. Number crunchers
3. Change agents
4. Front liners
5. Heavy hitters

Let's explore each one and how they can best help your company.

The Enthusiasts

These are your business development people. Maybe they didn't start in the construction industry. Perhaps they sold mortgages or worked for an architecture firm. But they love construction—and they're super enthusiastic about going out there and winning projects.

The enthusiasts are your bird dogs. They have their finger on the pulse of the communities you build in. Enthusiasts represent your company to new and existing clients. Their job is to meet people and notice new opportunities.

How can you best utilize and support these enthusiastic individuals? Be specific in delegating business development tasks to them. Using what you'll learn in chapter 12, show them how to stay in front of key clients and cultivate long-term relationships. Get them involved in those buying influences charts. This frees up your planners to plan and your builders to build. You can make sure they stay informed on important client dates like birthdays and anniversaries by using a shared calendar. Those details go a long way toward cultivating long-term client relationships.

You can also get your enthusiasts involved in local organizations, like your nearest Associated General Contractors of America chapter. Allocate time for them to join various boards and committees that let them get to know folks while serving your community in a non-sales capacity.

Now your enthusiasts do have some weaknesses. Because they're in business development, everything seems like an opportunity to them. And because many of them lack the technical chops you only get by being an industry veteran, they have trouble discerning a true opportunity from one you should avoid.

And let's face it, sometimes their enthusiasm can irritate your other people. Business development folks have two sales to make when they're developing relationships. Not only must they sell the potential client on working with you but also they must sell your team on working that project. Sometimes enthusiasts think that just unearthing an opportunity means everyone else will applaud them.

So how can you help enthusiasts overcome these weaknesses? Make sure your business development people have a clear understanding of your niche. They have to know the market you want to go after, the types of projects you want to build, and the types of clients you want to work with.

Take the time to educate them in the construction business by having them ride along with project managers to job sites. This way they can spend time with the folks in the field to get a better feel for the construction industry—including what your project managers want more of and what they wish they could avoid.

Help your enthusiasts bring new opportunities to the team. Give them some direction on whose buy-in they need to fire up your company.

The Number Crunchers

These are your estimators—the folks with plans open on one screen and an Excel spreadsheet on the other. They're good at accurately bidding work and getting bids out before they're due. They often have insight into engineering opportunities that can set you apart from your competition. Using that insight and accuracy, they build credibility with clients.

The challenge facing your number crunchers is getting out from behind the desk and selling that number to a potential client. Many number crunchers have the mindset, "I've got the number out, now I'll move on to my next estimate."

That's a mistake. One of my clients is an expert at working with his number crunchers. He reminds them that getting the number out is only half the job. They need to follow up by phone afterward. Even better, in person.

But many number crunchers aren't comfortable with that follow up. What if they make a mistake? What if the client challenges them? They need your support to develop the confidence necessary to interact with the clients.

Help your number crunchers' confidence in their knowledge and abilities by making sure they get the feedback they need from your team on the accuracy of their bids. This way they'll know where to make adjustments. They need you to communicate the relationship-building mindset that gets them actively selling their estimate to the client.

People don't buy because of the number. They purchase from folks they know, like, and trust. They want to work with people they have confidence in. Ensure that your number crunchers are making accurate estimates, and help give them the confidence to follow up with clients.

The Change Agents

Your change agents are your project managers. Many of them would look at you funny if you told them they were responsible for business development and sales. But think about it. Is it easier to sell a new client or an existing client?

Building a safe, high-quality project at a profit is challenging. When you do, you have the opportunity to deliver killer service to your clients. And if you can do that, you can build deep, lasting relationships that drive repeat business.

When you talk to your project managers about business development, think of them as change agents. Because often they're the ones selling the client on legitimate change orders that come up as you're building a project.

One of the key skills you can help your project managers develop is a keen sense of customer service. If you take care of your customers, they'll buy from you again and again. Serving your customers is the most fundamental business development activity.

Think of it this way: When an issue comes up on a job, it creates discomfort for everyone involved, including the project manager. So ask your PMs, "How much pain do you want?"

If they shove problems under the rug, the pain will increase. But if they act fast to provide excellent customer service with clear documentation, they'll minimize the discomfort for everyone. Addressing issues as soon as they come up helps cement a good relationship with the client. Your people's ability to fix mistakes increases the client's confidence in your whole company.

Work with your project managers to ensure they deal with issues quickly. Also make sure they don't air any dirty laundry when dealing with in-house issues. The client doesn't need to know how the sausage is made. They just need a high-quality sausage on time. Help your PMs emphasize customer service with timely, consistent, and clear communication, and your sales will benefit.

Also, specifically work with your PMs on how to negotiate change orders. Even when handling difficult issues, they should always be focused on building relationships. Instead of trying to get paid for every change that comes up, document the changes and communicate them to the client on a regular basis, like once a week. This practice builds a two-way obligation and lets the client know you've done this extra work.

The Front Liners

The folks in the field, your superintendents, your foremen, and your operators, are all your front liners. Because the field is where the money gets made, it's the front line of every profitable construction company. Even if they didn't realize it before, your front liners are selling the next project you build.

Everyone in the field is selling the customer service experience of working with you. When your field crews show up with competence, the people you're doing business with have confidence in you. This is a big part of making your construction company easy to work with.

I'll give you an example. I've been with Bank of America since 1988, when I opened an account in college. I've since opened a couple of savings accounts for my oldest sons. Bank of America knew they were children's accounts when I set them up, so they told me they wouldn't be charging them any fees. But what did I start seeing on my bank statement? A whole bunch of fees. And it really ticked me off.

So I went into the branch and told them about it. They said, "Oh, we'll fix it for you."

A few months went by, and they didn't fix it. So I picked up the phone to call Bank of America. It took me fifteen minutes to get in touch with customer service. After all that, they told me they would only refund three months of fees. The whole experience was a pain in the neck, and I had to tell them I'd be taking my business elsewhere.

In contrast, think about doing business with Amazon. Say what you like about Jeff Bezos, but whenever I have any issue with Amazon, they take care of it immediately.

Make your company difficult to work with, and your clients will take their projects elsewhere. Make yourself as easy to work with as possible, and you'll build those customer relationships.

I can't stress this enough—one of the key ways to sell the next project is for your front liners to be easy to work with. You'll build client confidence. Your clients know you'll get things done when you show up on the job site. If you have their best interests in mind, you'll build long-term relationships and secure profitable projects in the future.

Let's say you're a general contractor, and your closest competitor is bidding on a project. Both of you are bidding to a client. He's worked with both of you before, and your numbers are so close, it's a toss-up.

To help make the decision, the client decides to ask their construction manager how you performed on the last project you built for them. But they hear that your field team was a pain in the neck to work with. They communicated poorly. They fought with other project partners, and they underperformed in general.

So your client decides to go with the competition for the next project. Through poor customer service, your field personnel failed to sell the client on building future work with your company.

Don't let that happen! Teach your folks in the field to never forget that they're selling your company by the quality of the service they provide your clients.

You can create an on-site best practices operation manual to put in the hands of all your front liners. Have your PM and superintendent review it with everyone in the field before starting a new project. You can include things like speaking with respect, picking up all trash/cigarettes throughout the day, showing up on time, following all safety protocols, asking for help when needed, and sticking to scheduled breaks. When your clients see your front liners going above and beyond, they'll want to work with you again and again.

The Heavy Hitters

Your heavy hitters are the senior executive team, the final group of people responsible for business development. If you own or are a senior leader in a construction company, you're also one of the heavy hitters. The challenge your senior executives face is balancing their high-level internal responsibilities with getting out and developing future work.

Kings talk to kings. You know clients who want to look the senior executive, the CEO, or the president in the eye. This is why your senior executives must commit to building long-term relationships with existing and potential clients.

This is how you ensure your company's sales success in booming times *and* when the economic cycle dips. Even if you're doing well now, don't get complacent. The next economic downturn will come eventually, and you want to have developed those deep relationships with your clients ahead of time so that they'll look to you to help them solve their problems.

The best way to use your heavy hitters in business development is to divide your top ten to twenty target clients between your senior executives. Then you can hold them accountable for regular relationship-building activity with those companies.

Harnessing All Five Salespeople for Extraordinary Results

All your people must understand, whether they're in business development, estimating, the field, or the executive level, that everyone is responsible for business development—for sales.

My wife and I are still working on showing our kids how to clean the house. We remind them of their responsibilities and hold them accountable. You can take the same approach to harnessing the five types of salespeople in your business.

Here's how:

1. Identify the clients and project types you'd like your business development people to pursue. Clearly communicate this information to them.

2. Develop a step-by-step sales process for your estimators. This way they'll understand how and when to follow up—not just when they're putting a number together but after they've sent the bid to your client. Make certain you hold them accountable for completing this process.

3. Set the parameters of change order management with your project managers. You could also send them to a negotiation course to acquaint them with negotiating larger change orders. This also helps maximize your profitability.

4. Meet with your superintendents and your foreman. Have them do some creative thinking around this question: "In what specific ways can we win the next project by providing excellent customer service on our current project?" Then shore up your customer service and customer relationships based on the answers. Hold them accountable by following up with them each week.

5. Last but not least, commit as an executive team to spend a day or two each month in client-facing activities.

Follow all these steps, and you'll be primed to turn your company into a sales machine.

Not to the Swift or to the Strong but to the One Who Markets, Too

Now you know why people purchase from folks they know, like, and trust. They're also influenced depending on the four types of buyers in their organization. And that's just a small portion of building long-term, successful relationships in construction.

Closing sales is a skill. Like anything else, you have to practice. Approach your potential clients by using the buying influences chart as well as what we've discussed to get them to know, like, and trust you. That's how you make sure work keeps coming in, even when times are hard. Relationships count even more during the lean periods. So make sure you're connecting with the people in your client organizations.

But how do you *find* these potential clients? Where do you connect to new people to even start the process of knowing, liking, and trusting? That's where marketing comes in. And don't worry, marketing isn't as terrifying as everyone makes it out to be. You have most of the tools you need already inside your company. Next, we'll discuss how to put those tools to work.

CHAPTER 12

MARKETING: BE WHERE THEY'RE LOOKING

What is marketing? My friend Allan Dib, founder of Successwise and the author of *The 1-Page Marketing Plan*, defines marketing like this—how to get your ideal client to know you, like you, and trust you enough to do business with you.

The difference between marketing and sales is that, ideally, sales is one-on-one while marketing is how to do sales in a one-to-many fashion. Peter Drucker says that the goal of marketing is to make sales obsolete and to turn sales into order taking.

Most know how important marketing is. Few know how to do it well. And this is why so many construction companies struggle with outbound lead generation. Whatever business they get comes to them. When times get lean, that spells disaster.

Let me take the guesswork out of what may become your worst headache and show you how your company can put lead generation on easy mode. First, we'll cover the broad topics, then I'll break them down and help you digest. Once you understand them deeply, marketing will no longer haunt your dreams but give you an effortless stream of profitable projects that keep your business thriving in good times and in down economies.

Let's start with your brand.

Turning Your Company into a Predictable Leads Machine

The first question to ask is, "What's your brand?"

Successful brand marketers begin with the client. They talk to the clients and figure out why they buy. Once they get to know their client well, they shape the specific wording and broader marketing approach of their offer based on their client's needs. That's where the money comes from. Let's help you get it.

There are hundreds of thousands of construction companies in America. How are you different? What do you offer? What's your niche? Why should people in that niche choose to hire you? And how do they know about you?

To answer those questions, you need to understand your target market—the people your company is uniquely suited to serve. How much do you know about them and their specific needs? And how will you get the word out so that they realize you're the answer to their problems?

Learn as much as you can about their wants and needs, understand their frustrations, and be aware of how other companies have failed them. Where's their funding coming from? What are their long-term plans for the project you're building? What keeps them up at night? Why do they buy your construction services? What pain are they seeking to avoid, or what pleasure are they seeking to gain?

People purchase services or products to get pleasure or to avoid pain. In my experience, people will do much more to avoid a loss than to gain something. General contractors or owners purchase construction services so that the general contractors or the subcontractors will take away the pain associated with quality, service, schedule, or safety.

List all the problems your clients want to solve by engaging your construction services. Then reverse those problems and provide them with the solutions. If the problem they want to avoid is poor quality, the solution is good quality. If the problem is going over budget, the solution is staying under budget.

It's not enough to learn surface details. You must dig deep and understand the people who are looking for your services.

Try to offer guarantees. This can be tough for construction companies. But you might offer guarantees with regard to budget, schedule, quality, and so on. If that's not possible in your situation, don't sweat it. Focus on the other aspects of marketing.

Regardless, if you don't know your customers, you can't persuade them to hire you. Hoping, praying, and begging isn't a strategy. It's a recipe for disaster.

But it's not much help to know your clients unless you know yourself. That means finding and understanding your niche.

Nail Your Niche

Have you ever clicked onto a website while looking for a specific product, and it addresses your exact problem? You want customers to say, "Yes, that's for me. That's what I need!" They'll buy right away.

That's the experience you want for your customers. The way to get there is to nail your niche.

There is a wrong way to do marketing and a right way to do marketing. The wrong way is the eager beaver approach that has you out there saying yes to everything. That is the way many construction companies do marketing. They never nail down their marketing message.

One of the biggest mistakes people make with their marketing is wasting money and time on branding, design, and logos. I don't think anyone buys a construction project or engages with a general contractor—or even a subcontractor—because their logo is sweet.

Spending $20,000 on a visual rebrand and a logo won't land sales by itself. It might be part of your overall marketing strategy, but you should concentrate on how to spend a dollar and get a dollar or more back in profits from marketing.

That's why the right way to do marketing is to be laser focused, dedicating all your marketing efforts to the right job, right location, and right client.

Marlboro began as a women's cigarette brand. In the 1930s, their tagline was "Mild as May." At that time, Marlboro was perceived as feminine. They had less than 1 percent of the market share. At the end of the 1940s and into the 1950s, they switched their focus to men. They began by marketing their cigarettes with people like sea captains, weightlifters, war correspondents, and construction workers.

Then they hit on the iconic look of the Marlboro brand, which was the cowboy. Now when I say Marlboro, you don't think of "Mild as May," weightlifters, sea captains, war correspondents, or construction workers. You think of the cowboy, the Marlboro Man.

Within a year of switching from "Mild as May" to the Marlboro Man, they went from less than 1 percent market share to the fourth bestselling brand. The more they narrowed their marketing message, the more popular they became.

How many cowboys do you think smoked Marlboro? Perhaps many did, but there were many more noncowboys who smoked Marlboro. Yet the whole Marlboro marketing message was that cowboy image. It was extreme in terms of niche focus and success.

Marlboro succeeded in nailing their niche because they understood their customers. Here's how you can, too.

Understand Clients' Emotions

Taking the time and effort to better understand some key construction leaders changed my whole business. They began to approach me and explain why they purchased my services. Once I crafted my marketing message around the words they used to express those emotions, my business took off.

Let me show you how to replicate my success. Make a list of the top five to ten core clients you have now or would like to engage with. Request an interview with them and record it.

During the interview, ask them a variety of questions: What kind of construction solutions are you looking to buy? What are the biggest fears or frustrations prompting you to look for a solution in regard to a construction project? What's your ideal outcome, and how do you think you'll get it? Who are the last five contractors you've worked with? Which ones did you like or dislike the most? Do you consider yourself part of anyone's tribe in the construction industry?

You should also touch on some sensitive matters. What is your gender? What is your age? What is your race? What is your family structure? What is your income? What is your religious orientation? What is your political orientation?

You may object to this approach, but excellent marketers do this all the time—but not so that they can discriminate against people. They do it because they want to understand why their target market buys and to craft their messages around that target market.

In an advertisement for the 2021 Subaru Crosstrek, a couple describes what are ostensibly their children. But it turns out to be the three Subarus they own. The couple is white, they're in their early thirties, they're schlubby in a certain way. They have no kids, but they have three Subarus. Now think about that for a moment.

The ad is tongue in cheek, but it is specifically targeted. You can only be this specific in your marketing if you learn everything there is to know about your customer, including the sensitive details.

Ask yourself this question now: "How targeted is my marketing?"

You must ask a variety of questions to discover the core emotions that drive someone's purchasing decisions. You want to understand those emotions so that you can craft your marketing messages around them. Get with your team and make a list of questions from a marketing and a demographic perspective. Then pick up the phone and schedule those client interviews.

If you want to maximize profits, your marketing has got to be targeted. You must create campaigns that increase awareness so that the right clients in the right locations with the right projects know about your business.

Right Client, Right Projects, Right Location

Milton Friedman said the purpose of a business is to maximize profits for the owners and shareholders. Why do construction companies fail to maximize profits? There are three reasons.

Number one, they have the wrong clients. Number two, they have the wrong projects. Number three, the projects are in the wrong locations.

How do construction companies maximize profits? They have the right clients and they build the right projects in the right locations. It's pretty simple. However, it's easy to say and tough to do. How can you solve the problem of building the wrong projects for the wrong clients in the wrong locations?

You need to dial in your marketing efforts so that you are attracting the right jobs from the right clients in the right locations. You need to do this as an executive team. If you've never done this, or if you're not clear on it, sit down and meet with your executive team in the next thirty days to figure out the right jobs, the right clients, and the right locations.

There will be some who are the absolute dream customer for you. They're profitable, they're fun to work with, they value what you do. Then there'll be ones you don't really look forward to working with. Maybe they complain about the price, or maybe they're difficult to deal with. There will be someone within your current list of clients who is an ideal client, and there will be some who are not.

They will have many commonalities. It may be geography, demographics, size, or industry. If you understand who you enjoy working with and who's going to value what you do, you'll be very profitable at the end of the day.

Run a profit and loss analysis on your various customer segments. You'll find there are ones that are much more profitable, easier to service, pay on time, and not difficult to work with versus others.

Every dollar is not equal. Allan Dib calls it the principle of the unequal dollar. Some companies feel like they can't say no to any business. They think that all revenue is good revenue. The reality is that some revenue is polluted revenue. It is revenue that comes from suboptimal customers. They can't afford what you do. They complain a lot or they pay late. They're difficult to work with.

Then there are optimal customers who are promoters of your business. They refer new business to you. They don't complain about the price. They pay on time. A dollar from those customers who become raving fans, who are promoters of your business, and who are conspiring for your success is far more valuable than a dollar from a suboptimal customer who is not profitable and is difficult to deal with.

If you can concentrate on your optimal customers—the people who give you the most return for your time, money, and energy—you're going to grow your business far quicker than if you try to take all revenue on board.

That's why the best marketing messages attract some people and repel others. It's important that you, as a construction company, are willing to take a strong stand with your marketing message. Because that way you will attract the right people and repel the wrong people.

Now think about the right job and the right location for you. You will need to create a series of criteria that identify and define these right jobs and locations.

For example, one such criterion could be having a relationship with the general contractor or the subcontractors involved in the project. You might create criteria based on job complexity and job length. Perhaps you love complex projects that last one or two years. Or you might analyze the competition. Perhaps you're in a very competitive environment and you don't mind that because you stack up well against the competition. Or perhaps you want a job type that's unique. You may think of it in terms of meeting equipment requirements, having the labor force in place, or having a good project history.

Once you're done, you need to rank those criteria. Let's say you have ten criteria that make up a good job for you. Rank them from one to ten, with ten being the most important criterion and one being the least important.

Let's say you rank having a relationship with a general contractor or a subcontractor as a three and a particular job type that you build as a ten.

Then the total score will be thirteen. Add up the total score for each job type. That will tell you which jobs are the sweet spot for your organization. Go through that exercise with your key executive team so that you're on the same page for job type, client type, and location.

Once you understand the right job, right location, and right client, you can drill down to get more granular with your marketing. Let's get to some specifics like maximizing education in marketing, following the AIDA formula, and maximizing content. Then we'll tie your tools and processes together.

How to Maximize Educational Marketing

When I sit through a whodunit film, I'm clueless whether the criminal is the butler, the maid, or the professor. The same is true for many construction companies. When it comes to marketing, they know it's something they should do, but they struggle to figure out exactly what marketing is, who to market to, and what their message should be. It's all a big mystery.

That's why we're going to talk about how to attract your ideal clients using educational marketing.

Educational marketing is about nurturing a relationship by providing informative content. For example, someone who needs a commercial space may be researching land or may have bought land already, they might be hiring an architect, or maybe they're researching the types of buildings that are available.

If you can provide them helpful information that will get them a result in advance, then you'll be in a box seat to offer them that product or service.

It's like a chess master thinking three, five, ten moves in advance. Too many people jump to the end result, which is the customer buying from them. Like a chess master, you need to think through the likely touchpoints along their buying journey before they engage with a contractor.

Always think about the next action that they're going to take. In my case, I have the *Construction Genius* podcast but also a newsletter where

I teach subscribers how to turn their project executives into better leaders. Each email provides actionable tips, and many offer the opportunity to book a consultation with me. Resistance is lower because I've proven that my methods work, but more importantly, email newsletter subscribers who test them out in the real world have proven to themselves that they work.

There is no reason your company's website cannot do the same. From a valuable email newsletter to leads generated, deploy this education maximization tactic and watch business improve.

What goes for the online space goes for everywhere else that marketing is concerned. At every stage you need to think about the next visible, physical step that you want the customer to take leading up to the final stage, which might be the purchase. That's where you want to think through the whole buying journey, not just the end result.

A mnemonic device I've found helpful for mapping that journey is AIDA. Let me explain.

How the AIDA Formula Makes Marketing Turnkey

Does a particular area of your business fascinate you? Maybe it's a technical aspect of construction. Perhaps it's thinking of how your geographic area can be developed. What fascinates me is marketing. I've been in sales and marketing my whole life. That's why I'm always happy to learn about old marketing strategies that work in the modern world.

One marketing approach I want to teach you is the AIDA formula. It's a framework from 1910 that's still relevant today and that can dovetail with your marketing messages to attract and retain more of your ideal customers.

AIDA stands for attention, interest, desire, and action. These are the four stages of customer marketing. You start by getting their attention. Then you cultivate interest, push them into desire, and get them to take action.

What are you doing to get attention? You might take out ads in the local business journal or on LinkedIn. But are you standing out? People don't click on ads from random construction companies. They click on what catches their attention. A hook should personalize your company for them.

You can also gain attention by making moves that get your name out there. Anything that helps relevant people to see your work. Get your search engine optimization act together; be there in internet search results when users search for construction companies in your area. Sponsor commercial real estate events, or host a local entrepreneurs' networking group. You want your target audience to have a chance to see you and look deeper. If they never see you, you'll never hook them.

Once you've got eyes on you, how do you keep their attention? That's interest. Your identity and your accomplishments make you interesting. If you start rattling off numbers, you'll lose people's interest. What's intriguing about your company? What makes you different? If you don't know, it's time to develop your company identity. What are you best at? Share that and get your target audience interested. At the very least, make this crystal clear on the home page of your website and in all marketing collateral you send your people into the field with.

Next comes desire. What do your target customers want and need? How can you make their lives better? Show them the benefits of working with you beyond getting a building. What else are you delivering that the competition can't? Speed? Quality? A customized experience around their unique needs? What gets them salivating to hire you to build for them over someone else?

But your target customers won't act if you don't ask them to. Make sure you're asking for the sale. A call to action as simple as "We want your work. Hire us!" can be compelling. But saying, "We like work, so please consider us someday" is weak. People are more likely to hire an energetic company that's asking for the work.

Get attention, develop interest, cultivate desire, and drive action.

Remember AIDA when you write ads, give speeches, and connect in conversation. Use it in all your marketing. How do you grab a client's attention and hook their interest? Share some cool facts about your company that sets you apart. Cultivate a desire to work with you by relating beneficial outcomes that past customers have enjoyed. Then ask for the sale.

Maximizing Every Piece of Content

During lunch with one of my clients, we were talking about some of the challenges that he's encountering. One was handling the COVID-19 situation and the morale issues that some of his leaders were facing. They were demoralized because they had to deal with regulations, family issues, all that kind of stuff.

After that discussion, I went to my car, picked up my cell phone, and shot a video about our chat and some of the insights I shared with my client. It took me about three or four minutes. After that, I uploaded the video to Splasheo. Once it was captioned, I posted it to YouTube. I called it *How to Maintain Your Morale in Crazy Times*.

I like using video because it's a way for me to get a piece of content out there. I took the idea for the content from a specific conversation with one of my clients. That's an important insight to keep in mind when you're developing marketing. There is content for marketing in all situations that you and your people come across.

For instance, let's say you're dealing with an intense project issue. It might be threatening the schedule or the profitability or the relationship with your client, and your company overcomes that project issue. You need to turn that into a piece of marketing content because it's those types of things that will attract the people you're looking to sell to.

If you specialize in building a certain type of building, you should create a lot of content around that to help your ideal target market learn about it. Your website should have downloadable content that could inform a prospect and generate qualified leads.

In the case of my YouTube video, I posted it on LinkedIn, where it got 609 views. I use LinkedIn for most of my marketing. It's a very boring website, but it's effective. It's effective because when you connect with people there, it's more or less strictly business. We don't have to deal with the drama of websites like Twitter or Facebook.

One of the great things about Splasheo is that they transcribe my video when they caption it. I took the transcription to LinkedIn, and it became a popular post for me there. It received a number of comments, which I replied to. People shared the post as well, and I was able to thank them for doing that.

From there, I transformed it into a newsletter post on LinkedIn. Then I uploaded it to my blog. I also sent it to my email list and made it into a Twitter thread.

All this is from just one piece of content.

Remember, what people say about your services is much more impactful than what you say about your services. The best marketing messages have plenty of testimonials interwoven into them so that they build trust and confidence with the people who are checking you out to see if they want to do business with you. Getting testimonials is vital. It's easy to talk about how great your services are. But talk is cheap. You want word of mouth from your clients.

Call your clients, ask them questions about their experience with you, and get their answers. Record the call as well. Write up a draft for the client, send it to them, have them approve it, and there you have a testimonial. You could even do it via video. Post those testimonials on your website.

I have six questions that I like to ask my clients when I'm getting testimonials. If you'd like those questions, reach out to me via email, and I'll send them to you.

You might be thinking, *Eric, this sounds like a lot of work*. But it's not. If you have someone dedicated to marketing on LinkedIn, if you're doing one of these posts a week, that is totally sufficient. All you can do is to take that one piece of content and repurpose it.

Have a system for repurposing. For me, it's pretty easy. Once I've got it captured and I've got the transcripts, then I'm able to put it into a word processor and turn it into a blog post. You're not looking for perfection with your marketing. It's more effective to be sincere and genuine and to take on the issues that your target market is facing.

That's why it's so important that you tap into the wins and the challenges that your project managers and superintendents and foreman are going through on a regular basis on the job site and building projects.

Then turn that into content that is targeted to the people to whom you're looking to sell work.

Marketing doesn't have to be rocket science. It just has to be genuine, pointed to your target, and consistent. At the end of each content piece, include a call to action. It doesn't have to be a hard sell, such as saying, "Click here to send us one of your projects." Most of your social media, particularly as a construction company, is not going to be like that. Instead say, "If you have any issues, contact us." A call to action at the end of every marketing piece is crucial.

Draw from real life to create marketing content. Keep it simple, like a video or a blog post, but turn it into multiple pieces of content. Then include the call to action. That's how to maximize the impact of your content marketing.

The next step is tying it all together.

How to Use Testimonials to Power Your Marketing

Remember, what people say about your services is way more impactful than what you say about your services. The best marketing messages have plenty of testimonials interwoven in them so that they build trust and confidence with the people who are checking you out to see if they want to do business with you. So getting testimonials is vital. It's easy to talk about how great your services are. But your talk is cheap. What you want to do is get word of mouth from your clients.

Call your clients, ask them those six questions and get their answers. Record the call as well. Draft up a testimonial for the client, send them the testimonial draft, have them approve it, and there you have a testimonial. You could even do it via video. Post those testimonials on your website.

You might be thinking, Eric, this sounds like a lot of work. But it's not. If you have someone dedicated to marketing on LinkedIn, if you're doing one of these posts a week, that is totally sufficient. All you have to do is to take that one piece of content and repurpose it.

Have a system for repurposing. For me, it's pretty easy. Once I've got it captured and I've got the transcripts, then I'm able to put it into a word processor quickly and turn it into a blog post. You're not looking for perfection with your marketing. It's more effective to be sincere and genuine, and take on the issues that your target market is facing.

That's why it's so important that you tap into the wins and the challenges that your project managers and superintendents and foreman are going through on a regular basis on the job site and building projects. Then turn that into content that is targeted to the people that you're looking to sell work to.

Draw from real life to create content for marketing. Keep it simple, like a video or a blog post, but turn it into multiple pieces of content. Then include the call to action. That's how to maximize the impact of your content marketing.

The next step is tying it all together.

Tie Together Tools, Assets, and Processes

If you're ready to commit to marketing, here are three questions you need to ask yourself: Do you have the right tools? Do you have the right assets? And do you have the right processes in place?

From a marketing perspective, tools are things like your customer resource management system, your website, and your content management system. Your assets are the copy that will go on your website, such as an industry report or some other downloadable. Processes cover who's going to do what and when, on a daily, weekly, and monthly basis.

If someone opts in on your website and downloads a report, do you have the right emails that will go out to them in a sequenced manner? If you don't have what you need, plug that gap first. Create the tools and the assets necessary for content marketing.

When you're ready to produce a lot of content, next you must determine three things: who, what, and when. Who is going to create that blog post and how often? You might assign someone to create one piece of high-quality content a thousand words long on the first day of every month. This makes marketing a process.

Content marketing isn't necessarily a core competency of many construction business owners. You may need to outsource it. Allan Dib recommends that you have a marketing coordinator on your team in charge of content creation and marketing. If you get an outside specialist, your marketing coordinator will come in to manage the whole process and to make sure that they get the right analytics and the right cost per click.

The ultimate metric for content marketing is whether it is making you more money than what you're spending on it. From day one, you will need to have other metrics because there's a ramp-up period. Content marketing will probably not give you a return on investment from day one. You want to create a handful of metrics that are relevant for you or your industry. These can be metrics like website visits, opt-in conversions, marketing, and qualified leads that have been sent up to sales. There are three specific metrics that a marketing coordinator should track: website visits, opt-ins, and downloads of informative content.

Too many people treat marketing like an event, like something that you do once—one big splash or one big rebrand. That's where they go wrong. The people who win at marketing are the people who treat it like a process. They plan what they will do from a marketing perspective, daily, weekly, monthly, quarterly, and annually.

Testing marketing is also critical. You might think that a message will land with the audience, but you want to know what the target market responds to. You need data from actual prospects to inform decisions on messaging, pricing, and packaging. You need feedback from the market.

Today's digital tools make it far easier to test and measure on a consistent basis than ever before. There are website analytics tools that tell you if something's converting, and there are heat-mapping tools that reveal what's getting the most clicks. You have no excuse for not testing and measuring, because you always want to be optimizing your marketing. If something's not converting, you want to see why not and test something else.

Every day, ask yourself these questions: What have I done today to attract a customer? What have I done today to keep a customer? This should guide your strategy. Tying together tools, assets, and processes leads to powerful results.

Marketing Can Work at any Stage

You may be reading this chapter and thinking, *I wish I'd known this information before my company started hurting.* Maybe COVID-19 knocked you out of the game. Or you've been riding the downward slope for years.

Or maybe you're planning to start a construction company, but this chapter is giving you second thoughts. Yes, construction can be tough. It's also rewarding and just plain fun. Few industries offer the immediate satisfaction of driving down the street and seeing something you helped build—and knowing it will stand long after you're gone.

Marketing can help, but when do you do it? And what else should you be doing besides spreading your name? How do you get a company off the ground or out of the red and into the black?

I've got the answers—because this chapter is not the end. By buying this book, you've unlocked an exclusive bonus chapter—Chapter 13: How to Start (or Restart) a Construction Company. This bonus chapter is available only on my Construction Genius website. Visit www.ConstructionGenius.com/BonusChapter. Aside from the secret chapter, my site also offers the most up-to-date construction leadership, strategy, and sales and marketing content to keep you on top of your game for the rest of your career.

You'll also find links to contact me, follow me on social media, and gain new knowledge around the construction industry. I release a lot of podcast episodes to a huge and growing audience. Each episode introduces another expert who can help you maximize your profits while minimizing your burnout. If you're running a construction company, you need every tool you can get. Go to my website and enjoy those free resources.

Finally, thank you for reading this book. I hope you've gained useful insights that help you run the construction business of your dreams. There are enough bad companies in the world. We need more responsible owners out there upholding the reputation of construction businesses. I'm glad you're taking the necessary steps to become the best owner possible, and I look forward to working alongside you in the future.

See you at the top.

ACKNOWLEDGMENTS

This book is the culmination of a journey that began for me in 2004. That is when I first started working with construction companies helping them develop their leaders.

My first client was Lancaster-Burns Construction, Inc.: Jordy and Vance, thanks!

Along the way, many people have influenced me and helped me. Two in particular stand out: Bill Cole and Andrew Neitlich. Without what I learned from Bill, I would never have had the courage to launch my own business. Without Andrew, I would not have been able to grow it to where it is today. To both, thank you.

Finally, I owe a great debt to my wife, Nelya. Her faith in me and unwavering support as I've grown Construction Genius is an ongoing source of strength. Nelya, I love you. Thank you.

ABOUT THE AUTHOR

Eric Anderton is different from other construction consultants. Because most consultants understand business, but not the business of construction. Eric knows what makes a construction business tick. And unlike other authors, commenters, and podcasters, he understands the unique nuances of the construction industry. That's how he has helped countless construction industry leaders by logically breaking down complex leadership concepts into small components so they understand how to be more effective. And he has shared that information for years on his popular podcast *Construction Genius*.

In his new book of the same name, *Construction Genius*, Eric goes beyond the microphone to reveal the deepest truths he has learned about making a construction business work. Eric's high energy, vast experience, and simple explanations make building a construction business so simple that anyone can do it.

Eric Anderton has more than two decades of career and entrepreneurial business experience, alongside twenty-five years of public speaking, small group facilitation, and one-on-one mentoring. He is a trusted leadership advisor, executive mentor, and expert meeting facilitator for construction companies that range in revenue from $10 million to $1 billion. Since 2004 he has helped his clients increase profitability by clarifying their business purpose, building strategic plans, developing their best people, systematically innovating through obstacles, and executing their most important priorities.

Learn more about Eric Anderton at www.ConstructionGenius.com.